Historical Background
of The Doctrine and Covenants

by

E. CECIL MCGAVIN

LDS Classic
Paperback
Library

First published in the United States of America
by E. Cecil McGavin, Salt Lake City, Utah, 1949.

LDS Classic Paperback Library
reprint edition published by
Leatherwood Press 2005.

ISBN: 1-933317-01-9

LDS Classic Paperback Library is a trademark of:
Leatherwood Press LLC
8160 South Highland Drive
Sandy, Utah 84093-7403
editorial@leatherwoodpress.com

Copyright, E. Cecil McGavin, 1949.

Table of Contents

Chapter I: Joseph Smith Takes a Wife	1
Chapter II: Martin Harris and the Lost Manuscript	13
Chapter III: Oliver Cowdery Becomes a Disciple	32
Chapter IV: Whitmer Hospitality	47
Chapter V: The Elect Lady	54
Chapter VI: Thrusting in the Sickle	66
Chapter VII: A People Prepared	98
Chapter VIII: Joseph Smith Revises the Bible	124
Chapter IX: The Reformers Become Persecutors	141
Chapter X: The Land of Shinehah	145
Chapter XI: The Shaking Quakers	161
Chapter XII: "Ask and Ye Shall Receive"	174
Chapter XIII: The Vision of Glories	185
Chapter XIV: An Era of Doctrinal Development	208
Chapter XV: Revelation in Illinois	217

Also available in the LDS Classic Paperback Library:

Latter-day Prophets and the Doctrine and Covenants, vol. 1,
Compiled by Roy W. Doxey

Latter-day Prophets and the Doctrine and Covenants, vol. 2,
Compiled by Roy W. Doxey

The Vision or The Degrees of Glory,
Compiled by N.B. Lundwall

Early Masterpieces of Latter-day Saint Leaders,
Compiled by N.B. Lundwall

Secrets of a Happy Life,
by David O. McKay

Preface

There has long been a need for a volume which supplies the historical background of the Doctrine and Covenants. Most of the chapters in this modern book of scriptures cannot be fully understood and appreciated without a knowledge of the contemporary events, the environment, and the historical atmosphere out of which the revelations grew. Every chapter in the word of God to this generation came in direct answer to prayer. At no time were revelations thrust upon the Prophet Joseph Smith. He was always ripe for instruction and approached the throne of Grace through the medium of prayer before a revelation was given to him.

These divine communications are not extraneous, unrelated, unwelcome messages that were forced upon him. They all came as a direct and positive need for specific instruction to meet a special problem at that time of crisis. They are answers to prayers which were uttered at that critical time in order to gain divine assistance in solving a particular problem.

The Doctrine and Covenants is simply an outgrowth of the history of the Church. It cannot be separated from that historical movement. It is an additional witness and testimony, or a solution to a pressing problem which demanded an immediate and heaven-inspired solution. The book must be read in the full light of the historical movement of the time, else many of these divine messages become rather meaningless and ambiguous.

"Ask and ye shall receive," was often advised in the early revelations. Why the Prophet should be asking about these various problems remains a mystery unless one is well acquainted with the historical background and environment out of which these revelations grew.

This volume is not a commentary, nor does it seek to replace such a valuable volume, but to, supplement it.

This is a volume of history, gleaned from many sources, most of which are not available to the public. It has a wealth of material that has not been published in any general book before, illuminating the period and giving one a fascinating panorama of the interesting historical setting out of which these revelations sprang.

It calls back to life the characters, incidents, and environmental conditions at the dawn of the restoration and shows the pressing need for the revelations that were given at that time.

Everybody who has read the Doctrine and Covenants knows that a revelation was addressed to Emma Smith, the Prophet's wife, but it is not fully evaluated until one becomes fully acquainted with the "elect lady," and appreciates her jealous disposition and realizes how all her family and relatives were turned against her, and the abuse she was subjected to in her own household from her relatives, do we see any special reason or justification for a revelation to Emma Smith.

In the following pages one is given a speaking acquaintance with all the persons who were instrumental in laying the foundation of this great movement. The full scope of the history of the period is reviewed in connection with the chapter of God's word as the collection increased.

This volume presents the historical background of the Doctrine and Covenants, presented in a manner that will acquaint one with the full explanation of why the various revelations were given. When viewed in this manner, this book of scripture springs to life again. We realize a definite and pressing need for every revelation that was given and catch a full view of the historical panorama of the time. It enables us to see these divine messages as a part of the historical progress of the Church.

This book of modern scripture sprang from the matrix of Church history. When the full historical background is understood it becomes a living, throbbing volume, every chapter of which is understood and appreciated. The author has spent years of research in this fascinating realm of history and has written these pages so that others may better see the majesty and beauty of the Doctrine and Covenants by understanding its historical background.

This is not a book to be read from "cover to cover" at one sitting, but must be read in connection with the portions of the Doctrine and Covenants with which it deals. When a footnote calls the reader's attention to a particular Section, this book should be put aside at that time and the complete Section in the Doctrine and Covenants read before the perusal of this volume is resumed.

This volume must not be read apart from the Doctrine and Covenants. Its various chapters are but an introduction to the scriptures it attempts to clarify and explain. Every footnote herein is an invitation to close this book and read the designated material from the scriptures before another portion is read from this volume. By reading these two books alternately this volume will truly become a *Historical Background of the Doctrine and Covenants.*

                    E. Cecil McGavin
                    Salt Lake City, Utah
                    March 24, 1949.

PART I

THE NEW YORK AND PENNSYLVANIA PERIOD

Chapter I

JOSEPH SMITH TAKES A WIFE

A few years before the hiding place of the gold plates was revealed, there had been a mania for "peepstones" and magic crystal balls in the neighborhood of Palmyra. Many people became obsessed with the desire to use some peculiar stone as a means of gaining supernatural information and guidance. It seems as if a spurious agency were rampant in the community—the adversary working overtime with his cunning schemes of counterfeiting.

Every person who possessed a "peepstone" used it for the purpose of finding hidden treasure. Amid the haze of nonsense and error there may have been enough truth to keep the curious people believing in the "magic stones," but they were always associated with treasure hunting.

When the news had spread abroad that Joseph Smith had been told of the gold plates and the miraculous stones by means of which the record could be translated, many people regarded this instrument as a "peepstone." "Water witches," and "peepstone" gazers were popular in the mining camps of the area.

In the autumn of 1825 a prospector named Josiah Stoal came to Palmyra to purchase wheat, flour, and other provisions for a crew of miners he intended to put to work in northern

Pennsylvania. Upon hearing the popular rumors in the neighborhood that Joseph Smith had located some buried treasure by means of a "peepstone," he became interested in the young man and sought his assistance in the mining adventure he wished to carry out. He stayed one night with the Smith family and invited Joseph to work with him, but it as carefully explained that the young man was not a "gold digger" and would not attempt to use any supernatural power for locating treasure for anyone.

The prospector was fond of Joseph and persuaded him to enter his employ for the sum of $12.00 a month. They were soon on their way to Harmony, Pennsylvania, about one hundred twenty-five miles south of Palmyra. Stoal believed that the early Spaniards had worked the silver mines in that area and had likely cached some rich ore to conceal it from the Indians.

Arrangements had been made for the crew of miners to live at the tavern of Isaac Hale, which stood beside the old turnpike near the big bend of the Susquehanna. About the year 1790 Isaac Hale and his bride Elizabeth Lewis cast their lot with the pioneers on the frontier. They soon erected a large tavern for the accommodation of travelers and settlers in the area. Wild game and fowl abounded in the region. Since Isaac was an expert hunter and marksman there was always an abundance of fresh meat for the guests at his tavern.

Isaac was the most famous hunter on the frontier. In the autumn he would ascend the highest ridges and kill several elk while they were fattest. He made large troughs of birch or maple to hold the carcasses when they were dressed and cut up. He would finally fill the troughs with fresh meat and cover the meat with salt, above which he placed a thick cover of leaves and stones. When snow covered the ground he would convey the meat on sleds to his home.

Before a hand-mill was used to grind wheat and corn, there stood in front of the Hale tavern a stump mortar and heavy wooden pestle, worked by a spring pole. Each day the boys would grind enough meal or flour for the day's needs. The fruits of the chase and the primitive mill were exchanged with the neighbors for other supplies and labor.

At that time the tavern was a popular institution on the western frontier. Most taverns were a combination inn and saloon. The proprietors did not expect to make much profit from the hotel, but looked to their liquors for an income. The name "tavern" where liquor was sold was soon changed to "grocery" or "groggery," and finally to "saloon." Some courts in that area set the following prices before they would issue a license to operate:

"Each meal $18^{3}/_{4}$ c; lodging for each person $6^{1}/_{4}$ c; for each horse 25c a night; for each full pint of whiskey 5c; each quart of cider or beer $12^{1}/_{2}$ c."

Tavern signboards displayed such signs as these: "Whiskey and oats," "Entertainment for Man and Beast," "Food. and Drink," "Entertainment," "Drink While You Rest"

The Hales were orthodox members of the Methodist Church, pious and perfectly satisfied with the teachings of that organization. Isaac and his wife Elizabeth were as prosperous and successful as any of the settlers on the frontier. Both of them had descended from a long line of interesting ancestors dating back to the *Mayflower*. John Howland, the assistant Governor of Plymouth Colony, William Tuttle, ancestor of Jonathan Edwards, and many college professors, lawyers, judges, and other prominent persons were included in their pedigree chart.

There were nine children in the Hale family: Jesse, David, Alva, Phebe, Elizabeth, Isaac, Emma, Tryal, and Reuben. This family had its share of Bible names, an indication of their religious fervor. Emma was born July 10, 1804, and was twenty-one years old when Joseph Smith came to board at the Hale Tavern. In fact she was almost a year and a half older than Joseph. She was a large, well built woman, with dark hair, light hazel eyes, and a beautiful complexion. She was well beyond the age when most girls on the frontier married.

Joseph Smith was not yet twenty years old. A long distance from home, lonesome for his loved ones and especially his affectionate, devoted mother, he soon became fond of Emma Hale. In the evenings when the miners smoked and engaged in frivolous conversation in the front yard, Joseph sought the companionship of Emma. The family being naturally religious they had a few things in common.

Because of the rumors about Joseph's "peepstone" and "gold Bible" experiences, Emma's parents were very much opposed to the friendship that was developing in their home.

On Locust Hill, near the big bend in the river, a man named Beicher had found a queer stone by means of which he was receiving "revelations." A Methodist "class leader" at that place informed Isaac Hale that Joseph Smith was working in connection with Beicher. He told such a tale of falsehood that Isaac Hale became very exercised in the matter and bitterly opposed the young man who sought his daughter's friendship.

At an early time Isaac became an enemy of the young man his daughter was beginning to love. He magnified all the rumors he had heard, repeating them to Captain Buck who operated the sawmill near Stoal's diggings. Other trouble-makers who listened to Isaac's prejudiced reports and were turned against the young reformer were Tom Dimock, Zedekiah McKune, Levi Lewis, Jacob Skinner, and Oliver Harper.

In this environment the nicknames of "gold-digger," and

"peepstone gazer" were applied to Joseph Smith, names that were destined to be permanent in the vocabularies of his. enemies and carry a connotation of dishonesty and deception. Isaac Hale was not the least among those who sought to give that discredit to the young man who was fond of his daughter.

The Stoal prospecting enterprise was discontinued when a deep shaft filled with water instead of silver. Mr. Stoal returned to his home which was up the Susquehanna River about thirty miles above Harmony, while Joseph returned to Palmyra. He and Emma kept in touch with each other by correspondence, and occasionally met at Stoal's home for a brief visit. Joseph was always made welcome by Joseph Knight who lived in the same community.

During one of these visits in the home of their mutual friend, Joseph proposed to Emma. She later said that when she left home she had no intention of marrying him at that time, but he "importuned" her with such avidity "aided by Mr. Stoal, who urged me to marry him," that she ignored her parents objection and consented to marry him. She confessed that she "preferred him to any other man I knew, though my folks were bitterly opposed to him."[1]

They called on the justice of the peace in that community and were united in marriage on the 18th day of January, 1827. They were reluctant to return to Harmony, so were soon on their way to Palmyra. The house in which they were married still stands and was recently purchased by the New York Historical Society. A bronze marker tells of the historic marriage that was solemnized in that house. The name of the many non-Mormon writers have had much to say. about this elopement, but it ceases to be serious when we recall that Joseph was twenty-two years old and his bride was a year and a half older than he.

---

[1] *The Saints Herald*, XXVI, 289.

At this point we must pause to say more about Isaac Hale and his family, since their conduct had such a bearing on events that followed, including certain revelations that were given. Isaac Hale was, largely responsible for the persecution that was heaped upon the young translator when he began to dictate from the Nephite scriptures.

Emma's uncle Nathaniel Lewis was a "powerful local preacher." He and Isaac were determined to stamp out the "menace" at an early date. While Joseph was in Harmony in 1825 they had much to say about Joseph's delinquency and deception. "I'd like to try out the spectacles," the local preacher requested one day of Joseph. "I've got Clarke's *Commentary,* and it contains a great many strange languages; flow if you will let me try the spectacles, and if by looking through them, I translate these strange languages into English, then I'll become one of your disciples."

The reply occasioned much sarcasm and ridicule.

A few years later when enemies were collecting all the uncomplimentary stories they could find about the rise of Mormonism they found Isaac Hale a willing contributor. The notorious Philastus Hurlburt, while preparing his vicious book, Mormonism Unveiled, obtained a fund of information from the tavern keeper at Harmony, from which we quote a few paragraphs:

> After these occurrences, young Smith made several visits at my house, and at length asked my consent to his marrying my daughter Emma. This I refused and gave him my reasons for so doing. Some of which were, that he was a stranger and followed a business I could not approve; he then left the place. Soon after this he returned, and while I was absent from my home carried off my daughter into the state of New York, where they were married, without my approbation or consent.

After they arrived at Palmyra, N. Y. Emma wrote to me inquiring whether she could have her property, consisting of clothing, furniture, cows, etc. I replied that her property was safe, and at her disposal. In a short time they returned, and subsequently came to the conclusion that they would move out and reside upon a place near my residence. Smith stated to me he had given up "glass looking," and that he expected, and was willing to work hard for a living. He made arrangements with my son, Alva Hale, to go to Palmyra and move his (Smiths) furniture etc., to this place. He then returned to Palmyra, and soon after Alva, agreeable to the arrangement went up and returned with Smith and his family.

Soon after this I was informed they had brought a wonderful box of plates with them. I was shown a box in which it was said they were contained, which had, to all appearances, been used as a glass box of the common sized window glass. I was allowed to feel the weight of the box; and they gave me to understand that the book of plates was then in the box, into which, however, I was not allowed to look. I inquired of Joseph Smith, Jr. who was to be the first who would be allowed to see these and informed him that if there was anything in my house o. that description which I could not be allowed to see, he must take it away; if he did not, I was determined to see it. After that the plates were said to be hid in the woods...

The historian Blackman expressed the popular opinion of the community in these words, "Emma was intelligent, and that she should marry Joseph Smith, Jr., the Mormon leader can only be accounted for by supposing 'he bewitched her,' as he bewitched the masses." [2]

Isaac Hale never recovered from the disappointment of having his daughter elope with the young man he did not like, His family and that of his wife's brother Nathaniel, the "power-

---

[2] Emily C. Blackman. *History of Susquehanna County*, p.103.

ful local preacher," were such pillars of strength in the Methodist Church that it was a severe blow to their pride when they learned that Emma was married.

Isaac Hale's Will

Years later when he made out his will he seems to have forgotten that he had a daughter named Emma. He bequeathed to his "friend and wife of my youth, all personal property of every description." To his "dear son Alva Hale" was bequeathed the old homestead of ninety-seven acres of land. It was Alva's responsibility to pay to his brothers the sum of $25.00 "a piece." A paragraph obligated Alva "should he be able after paying his brothers as stated above and it will not endanger his freehold, to pay his sisters such sums as would be right and proper."[3]

There is no indication, however, that Alva ever saw fit to send Emma a paltry sum from his father's estate. In the Church, records there is not the slightest reference to any exchange of correspondence between Emma and her parents, They never visited the Smiths in Ohio, Missouri, or Illinois, and Emma never visited them. Her father died while the Mormons were enduring the persecution in Missouri, yet there is no record that she was told of that fact by a letter from her family at Harmony. The epitaph on his tombstone is interesting:

> ISAAC HALE, Died Jan. 11, 1839, at 75 years 10 months 10 days. The body of Isaac Hale, the hunter, like the cover of an old book, its contents torn out and stripped of its lettering and gilding, lies here, food for worms, yet the work itself shall not be lost, for it will, as he believed, appear once more in a new and beautiful edition, corrected and amended.

Her mother passed away in 1842, yet in the vast array of cor-

---

[3] Mary Audentia Smith Anderson, *Ancestry and Prosperity of Joseph smith and Emma Hale*, p. 303.

respondence that has been carefully preserved there are no letters from the Hale family. The Prophet's diary never mentions the Hale family, and it certainly contains no correspondence to or from the estranged kinsmen at Harmony.

Many years later most of Emma's brothers and sisters moved to Illinois, making their homes not far from Nauvoo, but they seem to have forgotten that they had a sister living nearby. Her sister Elizabeth manifested some interest in Emma's misfortune at the time her husband was martyred.

Elizabeth married Benjamin Wassen, and the family migrated to Dixon, Illinois. Since this was only a few miles from Nauvoo it gave them a good opportunity to visit with each other frequently, but the visits were not frequent. Elizabeth's son, Lorenzo, became a convert and was baptized by Joseph Smith. His brother Harmon and his sister Clara later joined the Church,[4] but Elizabeth never became interested in the cause her sister espoused. Clara married William Backenstos, who was a brother to the Sheriff of Hancock County, Jacob Backenstos. Joseph. Smith performed the ceremony in the Mansion House.

After the martydom and the exodus from Nauvoo, Emma's kindred did not become friendly with her, though for years she remained aloof from church activity. On one occasion when Emma and her children left Elizabeth's home to return to Nauvoo, she said to her fatherless child to return to Nauvoo, she said to her fatherless children, "I have no place to go but home, and no friend but God."

Twenty years after the rnartrydom Emma visited her brothers and sisters who were living in Illinois—David, Alva, Elizabeth, and Tryal. Her brothers were past seventy years of age, but their bitterness had not mellowed, with the years. Soon after this visit a tornado swept through the area, tearing a picket

---

[4] *The Saints Herald*, CXXXII: 465.

from the fence and hurling it through the body of Tryal, killing her instantly. Her daughter was seriously injured at the time. and died within a week.

After the Reorganized Church was started, the Prophet's eldest son, Joseph, visited "Aunt Lizzie" and her family at Dixon, while attending a church conference in that vicinity. He was disappointed because he was never invited to take part in the family prayer circle or say grace at the table. "Aunt Lizzi" preferred to have the prayers said in the old Methodist fashion. One evening there was a stranger in the house who was invited to say the prayers for the family—a new and embarrassing experience for him, yet Joseph was not allowed to participate in the religious devotions in the Wassen home.

Many families have later been converted to the Church after one of its members had married a Mormon, but this good fortune never came o the Hale family. The words of the Savior were certainly true of Emma Hale, when He said to His disciples:

> Think not that I am come to send peace on earth. I come not to send peace but a sword, For I am come to set a man at variance against his father, and the daughter against her mother, and the daughter-in-law against her mother-in-law, and a man's foes shall be they of his own household.

Persecution Up Palmyra Way

While Isaac Hale and "Uncle Nat, the powerful preacher" were denouncing Joseph Smith as a "gold digger and wife stealer," the same Satanic spirit was rampant up Palmyra way. The enemies were determined to get the plates as soon as Joseph should receive them. Eight months after his marriage he was given the gold plates. The night he received them he concealed them in a decayed log in the forest that crowned the hill. After they were taken to his house a few days later the enemy was always on the alert to watch for them.

One evening he removed the hearthstone in front of the fireplace and deposited them in the cavity beneath the large flat stone, which was scarcely replaced until the angry farmer folk burst into the house and made a desperate search for the records. Another time they employed a magician to bring his crystal ball to Palmyra and try to locate the gold plates. His failure did not discourage them, and there was constant danger of an attack at any time, thus making it utterly impossible to settle down in peace and translate the record in his own home.

When he was definitely convinced that it was useless to attempt to translate the precious record in Palmyra, he and Emma resolved to write to her parents and ask permission to return to Harmony for a season and share the hospitality of the Hale tavern. They were informed that they were welcome and that her brother Alva would take a team and wagon and set out at once for them. It is not unlikely that "Uncle Nat" and the Hales were anxious to bring Emma back and apply all the pressure of the Methodist Church to separate her from her husband. This generous offer may have been bait to lure her back into their influence for the purpose of breaking up the marriage. If we are to place any credence in the later affidavits of Isaac, this conclusion is rather forced upon us.

When Alva arrived at the Smith home on Stafford Street, and preparations were made for removing to Harmony, the gold plates were placed in a keg and covered with beans. The wagon was searched a few times before they got out of the state, but the keg was not opened. When they were made welcome in the Hale tavern and Isaac informed Joseph that he could not remain in the house unless he showed the plates to his father-in-law, then it was that Joseph became interested in real estate and made plans to purchase a small tract of land and live in the small shanty that had been used as a "pelt house." There was not room in the tavern for both families—and the gold plates.

From that moment it seemed that there would be no more peace and harmony by the big bend of the Susquehanna than they found in Palmyra, yet here the translation was soon to start, and here the opposition which Isaac Hale helped to stir up would make the task of translation a dangerous experiment.

Chapter II

MARTIN HARRIS AND THE LOST MANUSCRIPT

It is impossible to understand the story of the lost manuscript of the Book of Mormon and the revelations[1] that followed, unless we know the nature and personality of Martin Harris. For this reason we shall make an analysis of his life before we return to the Doctrine and Covenants and consider the revelations that were given concerning him.

Martin Harris was an unagressive, vacillating, easily influenced person who was no more pugnacious than a rabbit. His colleague Oliver Cowdery had a yen for the legal profession, but Martin would run to get away from an argument. His conviction of one day might vanish, and be replaced by doubt and fear before the setting of the sun. He was changeable, fickle, and puerile in his judgment and conduct.

His choice of a wife was an irreparable mistake. She was a strong willed, dynamic, aggressive woman who soon magnified his inferiority complex and made his domestic tranquility dependent upon his submission to her strong determination. Her relatives were of the same type and it was always a source of discomfort when they came visiting and gossiping at the Harris homestead 1. This was especially true after he manifested an interest in and a friendship for Joseph Smith.

---

[1] Doctrine and Covenants, Sections 3 and 10.

For years she was convinced that the new religious movement was a fraud. In the years that followed she reminded her husband of this conclusion when he mentioned the Smiths or manifested the slightest interest in the family. With the passing of the years he became deeply interested in the movement in spite of her desires, decisions, and decrees.

Without consulting his wife he often talked with Joseph Smith about his visions. The story of the gold plates made an impression on his changeable mind that could not be entirely ejected when he returned home and had to listen to the negative report by Lucy, who was supposed to do all the thinking for the family. Though he had been trained to be a silent partner at home, he felt free to think his own thoughts when he was beyond the sound of her voice.

When he learned that Joseph was soon leaving for Harmony, Pennsylvania he gave him $50.00, explaining that "I give this to you to do the Lord's work with; no I give it to the Lord for His own work." He was so unstable in his convictions, however, that he may have soon been sorry that he had given the money, especially when he heard the negative report by the party of the second part.

As he gave the matter further consideration, being tortured by his doubts and fears, he sought to apply the pragmatic test and get some tangible evidence to bolster his unstable convictions. Since he was not permitted to see the gold plates he thought it would be an assuring witness to have a transcript of some of the, strange characters from the metal sheets. Intent upon piling up all the evidence he. could accumulate to use as a weapon against the fiery darts of his wife, and other kinsmen, he asked Joseph Smith to copy a few lines of characters from the gold plates. He never explained what he intended doing with the sheet of characters, but his friend copied seven lines of characters on a small sheet of paper. It seems that on another sheet of paper he translated the seven lines of characters into English, giving to Martin the transcript as well as the translation.

The credulous, vacillating Martin showed the transcript to a minister in Palmyra, the Reverend John A. Clark, who later wrote a book in which he related this fact. He pronounced the characters as nothing more than "hen scratches."[2] This disturbed Martin painfully. He found too many people in Palmyra agreeing with his wife,

At last he resolved to settle the whole matter and make a trip to New York City at his own expense and get the opinions of linguists. Perhaps he had been invited to come down to Harmony as soon as he could get some friends to supervise the work on his farm, and become the translator's scribe. He was reluctant to accept that appointment until he had a stronger testimony of the work. He knew the price he would be obliged to pay his wife and other relatives if he should cast his lot with the unpopular reformer for a season.

At Columbia College he interviewed the brilliant professor Charles Anthon, who had mastered a few ancient languages and had written a textbook on the subject. The Professor recognized the root words that had a similarity to Egyptian, Chaldaic, Assyrian, and Arabic, assuring the farmer that they were genuine, ancient characters. Martin was so pleased to find an additional witness, that he showed him the translation of the characters. As the linguist examined the transcript and the translation he pronounced the translation correct, "more so than any he had before seen translated from the Egyptian."

After visiting another linguist in the city who confirmed what the first had said concerning the transcript and the

---

[2] John A. Clark, *Gleanings by the Way*, pp. 217, 222, 223.

translation, he was now fortified against all the fiery darts of the enemy, so set out for his home. This experience had made such a lasting impression on Martin that he was determined to assist in the translation. The transcript of characters was preserved, while the translation was lost. It was attached to the last sheet of the Book of Mormon manuscript which was retained by David Whitmer.

The sheet containing these characters is 8x3¼ inches. The word "caractors" that was written on the top of the sheet has occasioned much criticism. If an expert were to study the word carefully he would be obliged to agree that it is not in the handwriting of Joseph Smith. Judging from his style of writing, he simply did not write that word. The same careful examination would likely reveal that David Whitmer wrote the disputed word.

Soon after Martin arrived in Harmony a revelation was received which contained much instruction and information for the new scribe.[3] The Lord read his heart like an open book and encouraged him to be more humble. Aware that Martin was anxious to see the plates he was reminded that Joseph was to stand as a witness for these things and that he could not show them to others except as he was commanded. It must have been a source of happiness to be assured that Martin might see them in the future, if he should become sufficiently humble.

Years later Martin was the same unsteady character, believing a thing one day but doubting it the next. By the time the first edition of the Book of Mormon was sold he had drifted out of the Church. A few years later he had joined the apostate faction started by James J. Strang and went to England as a missionary for Strang. Again he changed his mind, left the Strang organization and was back in his old home in Kirtland, Ohio.

In the spring of 1828, Martin made a daring decision—he

---

[3] Doctrine and Covenants, Section 5.

was going to leave the spring work on his large farm for others to worry about and he would help with the translation of the Nephite scriptures. He turned a deaf ear on the arguments of his wife and kindred, and was soon in Harmony to serve as scribe. His wife soon followed him and demanded that he hasten back home, but he did not return with her. She searched about the place trying to find the gold plates. She sued Joseph Smith for trying to get money from her husband under false pretenses, yet nothing could take the new secretary from his divine task until the translator relieved him from the tiring labor.

For two months the scribe wrote as the translator dictated from the sheets of gold, during which time one hundred and sixteen pages were written in English. It was agreed that on the fourteenth day of June he would catch the stage coach and return home for a short visit. Since his wife and other opponents had importuned him to let them see the record he had written, he asked Joseph to permit him to take the copy home with him.

Inquiry by means of the Urim and Thummim brought an unfavorable reply, but the scribe would rather remain there than to go home empty handed and have to listen to the abusive criticisms that would abound in his own home. If he could but read the story to his questioning kinsmen he felt certain that it would give them a testimony of the work, as they realized that Joseph was not capable of dictating such a record unaided by divine guidance.

The second inquiry brought the same negative reply, yet Martin continued to call attention to what he could accomplish with the manuscript in his possession. After a third prayerful inquiry, the reply was favorable and he was permitted to take the document home on condition that he would show it to only five persons—his brother Preserved, his wife, his father and mother and his wife's sister, Mrs. Cobb. He took a solemn oath to keep this pledge and soon set out for Palmyra.

The next day the first child was born to Joseph and Emma, a boy who perhaps was born dead. No name appears on the headstone that still stands in the neglected cemetery near the big bend of the Susquehanna. For many days the young father was prostrated with grief. The loss of their son and the lingering weakness of the mother made this a time of sorrow never to be forgotten.

As the spring days slowly dragged their weary lengths away and Emma was convalescing well, Joseph began to worry about Martin. The time was past when he should have been back at his desk, but not even a message had been written to explain his delay. Joseph knew him well enough to know that he had likely been persuaded to, allow others to see the manuscript and it had been stolen. Ringing in his ears were the two negative replies, shouting disapproval of his plan. If it were lost the full weight of censure would fall upon his shoulders since he failed to heed the unfavorable reply that was repeated twice.

This was the beginning of Joseph Smith's career. Such a lesson as he would learn from this experience would never be forgotten. He must learn to hearken to the inspiration that came to him, and he must multiply copies of valuable documents. From this painful experience he learned *these* lessons well. In the future he had duplicate copies made of all important documents. When the translation of the Book of Mormon was finished he asked Oliver Cowdery to make a second copy of the long manuscript. When his revision of the Bible was completed he had a friend make a complete copy of that long manuscript and make the check marks in the Bible exactly as Joseph had done in the Bible he used during the revision. One year before his death he dictated the revelation that now appears in Section 132 of the Doctrine and Covenants. He had another secretary make a second copy of it as soon as the first copy was transcribed. When the one copy was burned he still had another copy safely locked in his office.

A few weeks after their first son was buried, the father was back in Palmyra where he learned that Martin had not kept his pledge and the manuscript had evidently been stolen. He rejected his scribe and went alone to Harmony, crestfallen and heartbroken. When he reached his destination his suffering was increased when Moroni took the, plates and the Urim and Thummim from him. Thus left alone with his torturing thoughts he had ample time to repent and let the bitter lesson sink deep into his heart.

He prayed that a more reliable secretary would be sent to him, as be began to feel that the task of translation would soon go forward again. He then commenced to worry about the manuscript that had been lost. Perhaps his heart would have been lighter had he known that it had been burned, but he was haunted with the fear that the men who had taken it had preserved it and would keep it for ulterior purposes.

When the gold plates and the interpreters were returned to him he received a revelation which explained the course the enemy intended to follow, and outlined the procedure that should be followed to defeat their wicked purpose. It was explained that these men intended to keep the 116 pages they had confiscated until the book should be published, then they would publish the short document they owned, after making many changes in it. Perhaps they would destroy the manuscript so that the alterations they had made could not be detected. This group of wicked men doubtless looked forward with great anxiety to see the book come from the press so they could print their garbled, adulterated portion, selling it for a few cents a copy and then circulate it in countless numbers among the multitudes who would delight in their nefarious scheme of deception.

The Palmyra preacher, the Reverend John A. Clark, had much to say about this subject. The following comments are typical of the opinions in that locality at that time:

> These pages were lost in the following way. Martin Harris brought home the manuscript pages and locked them up in his home thinking them quite safe. But his wife, who was not then, nor ever afterwards became a convert to Mormonism, took the opportunity, when he was out, to seize the manuscript and put into the hands of one of her neighbors for safer. keeping. When the manuscript was discovered to be missing, suspicion immediately fastened upon Mrs. Harris. She, however, refused to give any information in relation to the matter, but simply replied: "If this be a divine communication, the same being who revealed it to you can easily replace it." Mrs. Harris believed the whole thing to be a gross deception, and she had formed a plan to expose the deception in the following manner, Taking it for granted that they would attempt to re-produce the part she had concealed, and that they could not possibly do it verbatim, she intended to keep the manuscript until the book, was published, and then put these one hundred and sixteen pages into the hands of some one who would publish them, and show how they varied from those published in the Book of Mormon. But she had to deal with persons. standing behind the scene, and moving the machinery that were too wily thus to be caught. Harris was indignant at his wife beyond measure-he raved most violently, and it is said actually beat Mrs. Harris with a rod—but she remained firm, and would not give up the manuscript. The authors of this imposture did not dare to attempt to

reproduce this part of the work; but Joe Smith immediately had a revelation about it which is inserted in the preface of the Book of Mormon.[4]

They and their associates likely spent days planning how they would proceed and what a blow their course would be to the new society, but their efforts were only wasted. Though Satan was their silent but active partner, the Lord was not to be defeated by the enemy nor the slightest shame or discredit cast upon this American volume of scripture because of the use they would make of the pages they had stolen.

Another popular theory in Palmyra relates that when the five designated persons had seen the manuscript they told others about it and a small group of neighbors came to Martin's home while his wife was absent and insisted that he show the manuscript to them. This easily influenced man, vacillating and unstable as water, was exercised by their importuning. "We are good friends of yours, you have known us for years," they likely said. "You let Preserved see the sheets. Even Mrs. Cobb told us about the Nephites. Come, now Martin, be a pal and let us read "the story of Nephi."

Martin could not resist such arguments and for the moment forgot the pledge he had made to the translator, and let them see the document. When he was ready to put it away, one of the men had left the house, taking every page with him. Not a page of it was ever recovered. Years later Mother Lucy Smith dictated a volume about her family, She expresssed the opinion that Mrs. Lucy Harris burned the manuscript after she had read it, but this opinion cannot be true. The men who stole it still had it in their possession when the Book of Mormon "wabbled from the press on its calfskin legs."

There have been times when the Lord grants the unwise

---

[4] Clark, *op. cit.*, p. 247.

request of His children in order that they may learn through their experiences that their wisdom is very inferior to His. Ancient Israel demanded a king, but they were repeatedly warned of the dangers and the expense of maintaining a kingly dynasty. As they insisted that a kingdom be established, their wish was granted and after the long reign of three kings the united. nation was split asunder and two weak kingdoms attempted to replace the great nation that had prospered under the judges.

The loss of this manuscript of 116 pages is not without its parallel in Old Testament history. A prophecy given through Jeremiah was burned by King Jehoiakim. It was not only restored, but much material was added to the original: "And there were added besides unto them many like words," the scribe informs us.[5]

The Small Plates of Nephi

When the Nephites left Jerusalem they brought with them the Old Testament written on sheets of brass. They used that permanent medium as a model and made metal plates upon which they inscribed, their history. At the dawn of their existence in the land of promise they kept a dual history of their people, having made two sets of plates upon which they would record the events as they transpired.

The "small plates" were reserved for the religious his, story of the early Nephites—the accounts of God's dealings with them, the prophecies and sermons of their inspired leaders, and everything of a religious, sacred nature that should be preserved for posterity. Upon the "large plates" they inscribed only the political history, the secular, worldly incidents that were entirely devoid of the religious atmosphere of the Nephite pioneers. Until those two sets of records were filled with Nephite characters, the

---

[5] Jeremiah 36:32.

religious and political history of these early people were not intermingled at all, but when these records were crowded with characters they never continued the practice of a dual record From that moment forward the religious and political sketches were interwoven freely in the text that was multiplied on the many records they made for the purpose. Thus in the later chapters in Mosiah, in Helaman, Alma, and subsequent books we find a wealth of religious history and sacred chronicles, but at the dawn of their prolific record keeping they carefully kept the two accounts separated.

The small plates had been made by Nephi about thirty years after they left Jerusalem, and were handed down from one generation to another through the prophet-historians, being last written upon by Amaleki, who filled the last sheets with characters and delivered them to King Benjamin about 160 B. C.

After the Nephites had been in this land for a millennium they had accumulated a vast library of metal records. When the Lord knew that the apostate Nephites would soon be exterminated by the Lamanites, He instructed Mormon to make a set of gold plates upon which he should make a brief summary or abridgment from the vast library that had come down to him.

As he arranged his many records according to their age he became very confused about how he should proceed. His oldest record was the Old Testament inscribed on brass plates. He was told not to abridge that record, as the people who should read his epitome already had that volume of scripture. He then debated as to the best method of dealing with the dual record-the large and the small plates of Nephi. "Should I read a page from each record and then blend and weave them into one integrated account?" he likely reasoned. "Or should I save one sheet in my gold plates for a summary from the small plates and the next page for the large, or should I make a complete abridgment of one record and then abridge the other?"

Unable to reach a satisfactory conclusion he prayed for guidance and was instructed to abridge the large plates, the political, secular history, but was, not to abridge a page from the precious religious material. The small plates were to be put aside and not used at all in his summary.

Months later when his abridgment was completed and he was ready to go against the Lamanites in battle, he collected the many sets of plates that had been bequeathed to him. These were to be buried in the Hill Cumorah.[6] He was then commanded to take the small plates of Nephi which he had not abridged and place them with his gold plates, the Urim and Thummim and the breastplate. These were to be given to his son Moroni, while all the other records were to be deposited in the Hill Cumorah.

It seems evident that the four articles above were the only ones that Moroni later deposited in the stone box in the Hill Cumorah. Though the three witnesses of the Book of Mormon later saw additional records and sacred instruments, there is not the slightest reason to believe that they had been deposited by Moroni in the stone box he had made for the gold plates his father gave to him.

When Mormon was ready to place the vast library of his people in the Hill Cumorah, and was instructed to give the small plates of Nephi to his son Moroni, he explained that he did not fully understand why such a course was necessary, yet he knew it was for a "wise purpose" that the Lord was preserving the unabridged record that contained the superior and more important history of his people.

When Joseph Smith received the gold plates he also

---

[6] Mormon 6:6.

received the small plates of Nephi. When he began to translate he dictated from Mormon's abridgment of the large plates of Nephi. The portion that was lost was his translation of the abridgment of the political, secular history. When he was ready to resume the translation the Lord explained that "the devil has sought to lay a cunning plan, that he may destroy this work. . . I will not suffer that they shall destroy my work; yea, I will show unto them that my wisdom is greater than the cunning of the devil."[7]

Sections 3 and 10 should not be separated. They were surely given about the same time, as the one is a natural sequence to the other. The wrong date, May, 1829, has been given to the latter section. By that time the translation was almost completed. The small plates had been translated and put aside. In March, 1829, Section 5 was received, assuring Martin that he would be one of the witnesses, if he would humble himself sufficiently. This revelation was certainly given long after Section 10 was received. These Sections, 3 and 10, must be studied together as if given at the same time.

In the history prepared by the Prophet's mother is preserved the following account which gives a good picture of conditions at the time Joseph. gave this account of the incident:

> I commenced humbling myself in mighty prayer before the Lord, and, as I was pouring out my soul in supplication to God, that if possible, I might obtain mercy at his hands, and be forgiven of all that I had done contrary to his will, an angel stood before me, and answered me, saying that I had sinned in delivering the manuscript into the hands of a wicked man. and, as I had ventured to become responsible for his faithfulness I would of necessity have to suffer the consequences of his indiscretion, and I must now give up the Urim and Thummim into his (the angel's) hands.

---

[7] Doctrine and Covenants 10:12-48.

> This I did as I was directed, and as I handed them to him, he remarked, "If you are very humble and penitent, it may be you will, receive them again; if so, it will be on the twenty second of next September."
>
> After the angel left me. I continued my supplications to God, without cessation, and on the twenty-second of September I had the joy and satisfaction of again receiving the Urim and Thummim, with which I have again commenced translating, and Emma writes for me, but the angel said that the Lord would send me a scribe, and I trust his promise will be verified. The angel seemed pleased with me when he gave me back the Urim and Thummim, and he told me that the Lord loved me, for my faithfulness and humility.

He was then directed to translate from the small plates until he came to the point where his translation from the abridgment of the large plates had terminated—the ascension of King Benjamin to the throne. The same historical background was to be found upon the small plates, though it was clothed in an environment of sacred, religious, spiritual atmosphere. When his translation from the small plates introduced King Benjamin he closed that precious volume, opened the gold plates at the point he had last translated and resumed the translation from Mormon's abridgment of the large plates.

The first 132 pages in the Book of Mormon are taken from the small plates. The "Words of Mormon" are interpolated at that point, and the material that follows, is taken from Mormon's abridgment of the large plates of Nephi. A careful perusal of the book reveals that the early pages are actually a religious history, while with Mosiah we plunge immediately into the secular history of the Nephites. What a striking change in vocabulary, style, and atmosphere is apparent the moment we start reading Mosiah.

One misinformed writer has offered this erroneous explanation of how the translator proceeded after the 116 pages were lost:

> Consternation reigned at the Smith home when told of their horrible fate and, though Mrs. Harris later said she had burned the offending papers, it was always feared that she was keeping them for a possible subsequent use, A solution of the difficulty was found by continuing the translation at the 117th page. Thus the first precious pages of the 'history of Lehi are hopelessly lost to humanity.[8]

The Palmyra edition of the Book of Mormon contained a long account of the incident of the lost manuscript and what course he followed when the translation was resumed. This explanation covering a page and a half was never published in any subsequent edition. This paragraph is taken from that account:

> As many false reports have been circulated respecting the following work, and also many unlawful measures taken by evil designing persons to destroy me, and also the work. I would inform you that I translated, by the gift and power of God, and caused to be written, one hundred and sixteen pages, the which I took from the Book of Lehi, by the hand of Mormon; which said account, some person or persons have stolen and kept safe from me, not withstanding my utmost exertions to recover it again.

Few copies of the Book of Mormon were ever sold in Palmyra. The men who had stolen the manuscript were surely among the first to purchase a copy. With great anxiety they must

---

[8] *The Rochester Democrat and Chronicle*, August 4, 1938.

have taken it to their home, took out their carefully protected manuscript and began to compare the two as they completed their plans to publish the adulterated document as proof that the translator could not translate twice alike.

Their eyes glared ominously when they read that he had not translated the same record the second time, but had made the second translation from "the book of Lehi," or as we are prone to call it the small plates of Nephi. As one read from the manuscript while the others read from the printed book they were utterly amazed at the striking differences that appeared in every paragraph. Their plans had been useless; their project had been thwarted; their proposed publication would be the strongest evidence that could be found to show that he had actually translated from another record.

The adversary was again defeated. The Lord had triumphed and the Book of Mormon had not been cheapened, weakened or penalized because a few pages had been lost. To the contrary, the 132 pages from the unabridged record of the small plates were far superior to the introduction of Mormon's abridgment from the large plates that was lost, The loss of those few pages was our gain. The adversary and his agents had. not defeated the work of the Lord, but had been put to shame.

Perhaps the lost manuscript was not destroyed until the printed book came from the press. Surely the men who had stolen it discovered it the very day they read from the printed edition and saw the trap spring in their faces which had been set for another. This was a great victory for the Lord, a day of triumph for the cause of righteousness and a dismal day of failure for the enemy.

As the Church has acquired many of the historic landmarks near Palmyra, and valuable documents and a vast wealth of historical material have been uncovered, many have expected the lost manuscript to be found among the relics of a distant era, but the men who intended publishing it must have made sure that no one would ever see it again.

Joseph Smith was once asked why we call the Book of Mormon the "stick of Ephraim," while the book itself specifically declares that Lehi belonged to the tribe of Manassah. He replied that if we had the lost manuscript the mystery would disappear, since that record stated that Ishmael belonged to the tribe of Ephraim. It would seem that the blood of Ephraim predominated in the Nephites, while that of Manassah predominated with the Lamanites.

Though the enemy continued to consider the loss of the 116 pages as proof that Joseph Smith was not an inspired translator, but was operating in opposition to the will of the Lord, he hastened into the task of translation as soon as a new secretary came to help him, yet the enemy tightened their dragnets and became more anxious to put an end to his work. Because Isaac Hale, "Uncle Nat" Lewis, and others who were intimately associated with him, became such bitter enemies to him, it was almost as unsafe to translate in Harmony as it was in Palmyra. The name Harmony has since been changed to Oakland. There was so much disharmony and discord there at that time that it was purely ironical to call the place Harmony, yet here the first pages of the Book of Mormon were translated and many of the early chapters in the Doctrine and Covenants were received.

Two Book of Mormon Manuscripts

The loss of that small portion of the Book of Mormon manuscript made a lasting impression on the mind of Joseph Smith. In the future he would have a duplicate copy made of all important records. As soon as the translation was completed and Oliver had rested his tired hand, he was asked to make another copy of the long document. Many people find it difficult to read the Book of Mormon from cover to cover, but Oliver wrote it twice.

The original copy, no doubt, was reserved for the printer while the second copy was carefully preserved in case any of the original should be lost. The manuscript was taken to the printer in small installments; merely enough to keep the printer busy for one day, so that in case they lost a parcel of the document it would be a small one.

When the book was set up in type Joseph Smith retained one copy of the manuscript and Oliver was given the other one. One copy was placed in the cornerstone of the Nauvoo House, the other one fell into the hands of David Whitmer after the death of Oliver Cowdery. This one is now in the possession of the Reorganized Church. Not a page is missing and every word is legible.

The other copy did not fare so well. In 1882 Lewis C. Bidamon, who had married the Prophet's widow, sold some of the building stones in the Nauvoo House. When they uncovered the cornerstone they discovered that the moisture had leaked into the cavity, seriously damaging its precious contents. On almost every page of that historic document the ink had faded so completely that very few words were legible. Mrs. Sarah M. Kimball from Salt Lake City, Utah was visiting in Nauvoo at the time and was given a few of the best preserved pages of the manuscript. This valuable portion of twenty-two pages is preserved in the archives of the Church in Salt Lake City.

Years later Franklin D. Richards purchased several pages of the document from Mr. Bidamon, all of which have been added to the collection in Salt Lake City, though very few of the dim lines can be read.

There has been much discussion about these two documents. The writer has carefully examined the complete manuscript that is owned by the Reorganized Church and the faded fragment in Utah. It is not utterly improbable that some of the pages of the two manuscripts were mixed. The complete copy has several marked pages that could well be the printer's marks, while the rest of it is free from evidence of having been in the printer's hand at all.

When David Whitmer was interviewed by Orson Pratt and Joseph F. Smith he told them that the three witnesses signed their own names to the testimony in the preface of the Book of Mormon that bears their names. The complete manuscript does not have the original autographs, as they were copied by Oliver Cowdery. Though the manuscript is complete it certainly is not the original in its entirety, though it has been declared "authentic" by no less an authority than General Alexander Doniphan.

Chapter III

OLIVER COWDERY BECOMES A DISCIPLE

"My name is Cowdery—Lyman Cowdery—" explained a young prospective school master as he introduced himself to Hyrum Smith who was a member of the Board of Trustees of the school district that served the neighborhood not far from Palmyra, New York. After all the members of the board had interviewed the young man he was employed to teach school in the community.

A short time before the school season opened, however, Lyman Cowdery was calling on the members of the school board, introducing his brother Oliver and asking that they accept him as the teacher and release Lyman from his contract, since he had another position he preferred to accept. Oliver was accepted as a substitute teacher and soon entered into his duties as an instructor in the humble school house that served the rural area which included Waterloo and Fayette.

The Whitmer family lived in Fayette and the Smith's were soon to remove to Waterloo, after losing their homestead on Stafford Street near Palmyra. Oliver Cowdery was twenty-two years old when he commenced his duties as instructor, being almost a year younger than Joseph Smith.

At that time—the autumn of 1828—the farmer folk in that

community were still talking about Joseph Smith and his visions. Eight years had passed since his first vision; five years since Moroni showed him the gold plates; and exactly one year since Joseph had taken the golden tablets from their stone box in the Hill Cumorah.

The people who had grown up on the frontier, with the Smiths, their children mingling with the Smith children for many years, regarded Joseph Smiths accounts as flagrant deception on his part or that he had been deceived by the Devil. Oliver Cowdery was an outsider, a foreigner coming into the community. These miraculous events and all the characters in connection with them were viewed by him with an open mind. He was free from the popular prejudices and provincial jealousies of the neighborhood. While his informants laughed and ridiculed as they recited the local history to the visiting school master, he did not share their spirit of frivolity. Sober minded and serious by nature, he lent a willing ear to the tales he heard about Joseph Smith, insisting that the pragmatic test should be applied.

The school master had occasion to visit frequently with the parents of his pupils, most of whom doubtless took upon themselves the responsibility of keeping him informed on the most popular gossip in the community. It was customary in many rural sections at that early date for the teacher to board with the parents of the children who attend his school. This accommodation served as the major, portion of his recompense for "keeping the school," and gave him an opportunity to become acquainted with the domestic environment and parental background of his pupils.

One teacher during that pioneer period has left us the following vivid and humorous account of boarding with the parents of his pupils:

BOARDING ROUND IN VERMONT

MONDAY. Went to board at Mr. B's, had a baked gander for dinner, suppose from its size, the thickness of the skin and other venerable appearances it must have been one of the first settlers in Vermont; made a slight impression on the patriarch's breast. Supper—cold gander and potatoes. Family consists of the man, good wife, daughter Peggy, four boys, Pompey the dog, and a brace of cats. Fire built in the square room about nine o'clock, and a pile of wood lay by the fireplace; saw Peggy scratch her fingers, and couldn't take the hint; felt squeemish about the stomach, and talked of going to bed; Peggy looked sullen, and put out the fire in the square room; went to bed, and dreamed of having eaten a quantity of stone wall.

TUESDAY. Cold gander for breakfast, swamp tea and nut cake—the latter some consolation. Dinner—the legs, etc., of the gander, done up warm, one nearly despatch. Supper—the other leg, etc, cold. Went to bed as Peggy was carrying in the fire to the square room; dreamed I was a mud turtle, and got on my back and could not get over again.

WEDNESDAY. Cold gander for breakfast; complained of sickness, and could eat nothing. Dinner—wings, etc, of the gander warmed up; did' my best to destroy them, for fear they should be left for supper; did not succeed; dreaded supper all afternoon. Supper—hot Johnny cake; felt greatly relieved; thought I had got clear of the gander and went to bed for a good night's rest; disappointed; very cool night, and couldn't keep warm; got up and stopped the broken window with my coat and vest; no use; froze the tip of my nose and one ear before morning.

THURSDAY. Cold gander again; much discouraged to see

the gander not half gone; went visiting for dinner and supper; slept abroad and had pleasant dreams.

FRIDAY. Breakfast abroad. Dinner at Mrs. B's; cold gander and potatoes—the latter very good; ate them and went to school quite contented. Supper—Cold gander and no potatoes, bread heavy and dry; had the headache and couldn't eat. Peggy much concerned; had a fire built in a square room, and thought she and I had better sit there out of the noise; went to bed early; Peggy thought too much sleep bad for the headache.

SATURDAY. Cold gander and hot Indian Johnny cake; did very well. Dinner—cold gander again; didn't keep school this afternoon; weighed and found I had lost six pounds the last week; grew alarmed; had a talk with Mr. B. and concluded I had boarded out his share.

Peter Whitmer's large and hospitable home was often the abiding place of Oliver Cowdery, There were eight children in the family, some of whom were his students. David was the same age as Oliver and they soon became devoted friends. The parents were fond of Oliver from the moment they made his acquaintance. They took delight in the fact that he showed special attention and affection to their daughter, Elizabeth Ann. The whole family looked upon him as a man without guile; unassuming, unswerving, his thoughts and conversation at pure and refined as that of a modest girl's.

Because of the lasting impression Oliver made on the Whitmer family and the deep interest they had in him before the school term closed in the spring of 1829, we should interpolate that Oliver Cowdery and Elizabeth Ann Whitmer were married in Jackson County, Missouri, on December 18, 1832. This was the first marriage within the Church in the state of Missouri.

This explains in a large measure the abiding interest the Whitmers manifested in Oliver Cowdery, and why they played such a prominent part in the new Church which was soon to be organized in their home.

From School Master to Secretary

For many months Oliver had listened to the gossip about Joseph Smith and his visions, but they made a greater impression upon this open minded visitor than they did upon most of the local citizens. He gave thoughtful and prayerful attention to every rumor he heard. When springtime called the farmer boys into the fields and the forests and the little school house was closed for the summer months, Oliver was free to make a thorough investigation of the subject.

By that time his friendship for David equaled that which Jonathan manifested for another David in ancient Israel. He had endeared himself to the entire Whitmer family. Elizabeth Ann, perhaps, was dreaming of the day when she might become his bride, and all the family shared her dream.

Oliver had become so exercised by the provincial and prejudiced rumors he had heard that he was determined to investigate the matter himself. It was agreed that he should be a delegate representing the Whitmer family, and make the long journey down to Harmony, Pennsylvania and interview Joseph Smith. The results of his investigation would be eagerly awaited by all the Whitmers. Late in March the school doors were locked and Oliver was free for the summer. Perhaps Oliver had boarded for a season with the Smith family and had been favorably impressed with their account of "the marvelous work and a wonder."

Joseph's younger brother Samuel with one of the Smith teams and wagons took Oliver from Palmyra to Harmony. The wagon surely carried a supply of food, clothing, and provisions to sustain life so that the translator would not need to neglect his holy work in order to provide a livelihood at that time. The fact that the Smiths would furnish transportation for Oliver was evidence that they knew him well and had the utmost confidence in him. It was a journey of one hundred and twenty-five miles through the "wilderness" and along the beautiful Susquehanna to the Hale tavern near the "big bend" in that majestic river.

Samuel remained in Harmony for several weeks. He was the third person baptized in this dispensation, being baptized just ten days after the appearance of John the Baptist.

As the first Sabbath in April drew to a close, Oliver Cowdery was introduced to Joseph Smith in the Hale tavern near the big bend of the Susquehanna. "My natural eyes for the first time beheld this brother," he later wrote of the occasion. From that moment he felt amply rewarded for the journey he had made, and he was convinced that Joseph Smith was no deceiver.

All doubts vanished when Joseph Smith received a revelation addressed to Oliver,[1] in which mention was made of the fact that Oliver had prayed for a testimony of this work. He had never confessed this fact to his most intimate friend, yet Joseph Smith calls it to his attention. From, that moment he was a devoted disciple. He ceased to think about the little school house up Palmyra way or his old plans of continuing his studies. He had found the pearl of great price and was now, ready "to thrust in his sickle with his might and reap while the day lasts."

They spent the following day in conversation. This was a day of Pentecostal feasting. Oliver's questions had all been answered and he had a burning testimony that Joseph Smith was certainly a man of God. He was thrilled beyond description when he was invited to remain in Harmony and become the prophet's

---

[1] Doctrine and Covenants, Section 8.

scribe. To be associated with such a leader in such a promising movement thrilled his tender heart and caused his "bosom to burn."

Two days after he crossed the threshold of the Hale tavern he was seated beside his esteemed friend, writing the account of Lehi's preparations to leave Jerusalem. "These were days never to be forgotten—to sit under the sound of a voice dictated by the inspiration of heaven, awakened the utmost gratitude of this bosom," he later wrote of this experience.

As soon as he gained a testimony of the work he wrote a letter to his beloved friend David, giving him a full account of his startling discoveries. As a delegate of that family he was in a position to influence them regarding this unpopular movement. The Whitmers reacted favorably to his discovery and soon offered the hospitality of their home as a refuge for Joseph and Oliver who could find no other place in which to accomplish their work.

Soon after Joseph and Emma returned to Harmony, they purchased from Isaac Hale about thirteen acres of land back of his homestead. They lived in the small cabin not far from the large tavern, which Isaac had used as a "pelt house" in which he skinned the hides from the animals he killed in the forest. During the winter months he often had several deer carcasses hanging in the back room of the cabin, while pelts, traps, guns, and antlers were strewn about the front room.

In this humble shack the first pages were translated of that strange book which was destined to become the second best seller in the world, appearing in twenty languages one hundred and twenty years hence, springing from the press at the rate of 35,000 copies a year after nearly 2,000,000 copies had been sold during the years.

Every day there were experiences in that humble environment that confirmed Oliver's convictions, giving him additional evidence that his friend was a great seer and prophet. In one of their early discussions they failed to agree on the question of the translation of John. Oliver was astonished when Joseph inquired of the Lord and a revelation cleared up the mystery.[2]

Experiences like these soon convinced Oliver that he had found a man of God. This historic document that was given at this time was a translation of the account John had written himself centuries before. The parchment was not in Joseph's possession. By means of the Urim and Thummim he saw the ancient manuscript as John had written it, though it may have since been destroyed.

The content of this revelation was sufficient to make a profound impression on Oliver's eager mind, but to read a recent translation of an ancient manuscript in John's handwriting, answering such a vital question must have given him a powerful testimony that he was in the presence of an inspired man.

The Christian world has long awaited such corroborative evidence. If the original manuscript had been found by some scholars and translated for this generation to read it would have been hailed as the most important discovery that had been made for centuries, The value of such documents as this revelation was expressed by the Reverend John Watson in these words:

> Were a parchment discovered in an Egyptian mound, six inches square, containing fifty words which were certainly spoken by Jesus, this utterance would account more than all the books which have been published since the first century. If a veritable picture of the Lord could be unearthed from a catacomb, and the world could see with its own eyes what he was like, it would not matter that its colors were faded, and that it was roughly drawn, that picture would have at once a solitary place amid the treasures of art. [3]

---

[2] Doctrine and Covenants, section 7.
[3] John Watson. *Life of the Master*, Prologue.

The historian George Rawlinson expressed the views of millions when he wrote these lines:

> It is a happy omen, that, while so much of the literature of our times is marked by a tone of infidelity, and especially by a disparagement of the evidences of the authenticity and inspiration of the Scriptures, there is in other quarters an increasing readiness to make the choicest gifts of modern science and learning tributary to the word of God. The eclipse of faith is not total. And it is an additional cause of gratitude to the God of Providence and of Revelation, that even at this remote distance of time from the date of the Sacred Grades, new evidence of their credibility and accuracy are continually coming to light. How much may yet remain buried under barren mounds, or entombed in pyramids and catacombs, or hidden in the yet unexplored pages of some ancient literature, it were vain to conjecture, but of this we may be sure, that if any new forms of evidence should hereafter be needed, to meet any new forms of unbelief, and authenticate afresh the word of truth, they will be found deposited somewhere, waiting for the fullness of, time; and God will bring them forth in their season, from the dark hieroglyphics, or the desert sands, or the dusty manuscripts, to confound the adversaries of his word, and to "magnify it above all his name."4

Before Oliver arrived in Harmony, the Prophet's father had made the long trip down the Susquehanna to take provisions, clothing and what little money could be raised for the purpose. He must have felt well repaid for his journey when his son dictated a revelation in his behalf.5

No friend of the new dispensation was more deserving of a revelation than Joseph's faithful father, who had always manifested explicit faith in his son's mission. He was baptized the day the

---

4 Quoted in B. H. Roberts. *New Witnesses for God*, II, Foreword.
5 Doctrine and Covenants, Section 4.

Church was organized, was later ordained the Patriarch to the Church, and the President of the high priesthood. He was one of the stalwart pillars of the Church, never wavering for a moment. On September 14, 1840 he died from tuberculosis which had been brought on by the hardships he suffered in Missouri.

"To sit under the sound of a voice dictated by the inspiration of heaven," inspired Oliver with a desire to translate himself. What a thrill it would be for this new convert to catch the vision from the Reformed Egyptian characters and repeat in English the hidden secrets they concealed.

Since the gold plates were not to be shown to anyone until a revelation should dictate it, the scribes were not allowed to see the record. from which the translation was made. A curtain was drawn between the two tables at which the translator and his secretary were seated. A heavy cloth bag was made for the purpose of concealing them. At meal time or when they left the room for exercise the plates were placed in the bag. At the close of the day they were locked in a box which was prepared for that purpose.

A short time before Emma Smith passed away she told her sons that she had felt the plates while they were in the cloth bag, having lifted a few of the sheets and letting them fall with a dull, metallic thud. She repeated that she was never permitted to see them, however, though the box containing them was often kept under the bed on which she slept. Day after day as the scribe listened to the voice of the translator he became anxious to share the gift of translation. Perhaps reluctantly he made his wishes known and after a prayerful inquiry he was given permission to translate. It is not unlikely that a few lines of characters were transcribed from the gold plates and the secretary was permitted to experiment on that fresh manuscript. As he stared at the illegible characters they. failed to awaken from their long slumber. He expected a miraculous transformation of flesh and sinew to call back the sleeping skeletons from the past and clothe them with modern meaning, but nothing appeared before his eyes but those meaningless marks of antiquity. No inspiration from within supplied him with modern synonyms for those unknown characters from out of the past.

In utter despair and disappointment he sought consolation from his instructor. Again the prayerful inquiry brought the answer.[6] This explanation contained, the key to the secret of translation, at least about the only key that has been given to explain this mystery. "You have supposed that I would give it unto you, when you took no thought, save it was to ask me... you must study it out in your own mind; then you must ask me if it be right, and if it is right I will cause that your bosom shall burn within you; therefore, you shall feel that it is right."

Joseph Smith never fully explained the art of translation. On one occasion a few of the leaders of the Church were assembled in meeting and Hyrum Smith invited his brother to explain to them just how he translated from the Nephite records. This request was ignored and not a word of explanation was offered. Except for this brief explanation we stand as baffled as Oliver Cowdery was when his desire to translate. was not achieved.

Intimate friends called at 'the little cabin behind the Hale tavern to visit with the translator and learn how he was progressing. Two such friends were given blessings at that time which have been preserved. They were Hyrum Smith and Joseph Knight.[7] These friends brought provisions and supplies so that, the work of translation would go forward without delay.

The climax to Oliver's early career in the work of the Lord was on that historic day; May 15, 1829, when they were dis-

---

[6] Doctrine and Covenants, Sections 8 and 9.
[7] Doctrine and Covenants, Sections 11 and 12.

cussing the subject of baptism. They had read that the Nephites practiced the ordinance of baptism. Since they had not been baptized they sought further information on this important question. In response to their supplication John the Baptist appeared and conferred upon them the keys of the Aaronic Priesthood.[8]

In the *Messenger and Advocate* a few years later Oliver Cowdery published this comment:

> On a sudden, as, from the midst of eternity, the voice of the Redeemer spake peace to us, while the veil was parted and the angel of God came down clothed with glory, and delivered the anxiously looked for message, and the keys of the gospel of repentance. What joy! what wonder! what amazement! While the world was racked and distracted—while millions were groping as the blind for the wall, and while all men were resting upon uncertainty as a general mass, our eyes beheld—our ears heard, as in the blaze of day; yes, more, above the glitter of the May sunbeam, which then shed its brilliancy over the face of nature. Then his voice, though mild, pierced to the center, and his words, "I am they fellow-servant," dispelled every fear. We listened—we gazed—we admired. 'Twas the voice of the angel from glory; 'twas a message from the Most High. And as we heard we rejoiced, while his love enkindled upon our souls, and we were wrapped in the vision of the Almighty. Where was room for doubt? No where; uncertainty had fled; doubt had sunk, no more to rise, while fiction and deception had fled forever.

This was the last revelation given in Harmony until the translation was completed and the Book of Mormon was on the press, at which time Joseph returned to Harmony and further revelations were received while he was there.[9] For the present their mission in Harmony was terminated, as greener pastures loomed on the horizon.

---

[8] Doctrine and Covenants, Section 13.
[9] Doctrine and Covenants, Sections 24, 25, 26, and 27.

It was customary for Joseph Smith to record in his diary an appraisal of his intimate friends. Time has proved that these comments were similar to inspired patriarchal blessings. He read the hearts of his friends as if they were open books. Concerning his dear friend Oliver he wrote these lines at an early date.

> Beloved of the Lord is Brother Oliver, nevertheless there are two evils in him that he must needs forsake or he cannot altogether escape the buffittings of the adversary. If he shall forsake these evils he shall be forgiven and shall be made like unto the bow which the Lord hath set in the heavens. He shall be a sign and an ensign unto the nations; behold he is blessed of the Lord for his constancy, and steadfastness in the work of the Lord, wherefore he shall be blessed in his generation and they shall never be cut off and he shall be blessed out of many troubles and if he keep the commandments aid hearkens unto the council of the Lord, his rest shall be glorious.

Though he did not describe the two evils that must be overcome, we must conclude that those faults were never conquered. In the passing years Oliver did not measure up to the responsibilities that were thrust upon him. "He shall be blessed in his generation and they shall never be cutoff," was a remarkable conditional promise. Such promises are to be fulfilled in proportion to the person's faithfulness.

Because of Oliver's delinquency his generation has been cut off. This great man who stood shoulder to shoulder with Joseph Smith at the dawn of the restoration is left without posterity. His seed has been cut off because he did not do his part in fulfilling the contract.

Six children were born to Oliver and Elizabeth Ann, all of whom but one died in early infancy. Their daughter, Marie Louise grew to maturity, married Dr. Charles Johnson, but died without leaving children to perpetuate the Cowdery name or "generation".

Elizabeth Ann was only thirty-five years old when her husband passed away, but she never remarried. After her daughter's marriage she made her home in the Johnson home. An abiding friendship and devotion grew with the passing years. Their hearts became entwined in friendship. So devoted were they that when the mother passed away, January 2, 1892, the daughter died one week later. At that moment the "second elder's of the Church was left without posterity. "How blessings vanish when men from God have strayed."

It should be stated that after Oliver had been out of the Church for ten years he returned. While the exodus from Nauvoo was in progress he journeyed to Kanesville, on the east bank of the Missouri. At a meeting in the log tabernacle at that popular rendezvous he made the following speech which reveals the feelings of his heart at that time:

> Brethren, for a number of years I have been separated from you. I now desire to come back. I wish to come humbly and to be one in your midst. I seek no station; I only wish to be identified with you. I am out of the Church. I am not a member of it. I wish to come in at the door. I know the door. I have not come here to seek precedence. I come humbly and throw myself upon the decisions of this body, knowing as I do that its decisions are right and should be obeyed.

If Oliver had remained faithful, standing shoulder to shoulder with the Prophet, always upholding his hands and. sustaining him through those troublesome years in Ohio, Missouri, and Illinois, his name would have been carried the ends of the earth as the "second elder" of the Church. He would have remained second only to his great leader. According to the eternal law of witnesses and testimony he likely would have gone to Carthage with his master where the seal of martyrdom would have been written with his own life's blood. By that same immutable law Hyrum Smith was called to take Oliver's place as a witness. All the blessings that had been promised to Oliver were pronounced upon the head of Hyrum. While Oliver is without posterity in the earth, Hyrum's seed is numbered by the hundreds.

Oliver returned to the Church in October, 1848. He spent much time laboring with the Whitmers, persuading them to follow the light and return to the Church in which they played such a prominent part as the light of the restoration burst upon the world. He passed away March 3, 1850, at Richmond, Missouri, where most of the Whitmers then resided. His last moments were spent in bearing testimony of the truthfulness of the Gospel. His last words were these, "Lay me down, and let me fall asleep."

Chapter IV

WHITMER HOSPITALITY

After Martin Harris had lost the manuscript he had copied, it tended to turn the enemy against the work more than. they had been before. When Joseph related that the angel had taken the plates and the sacred interpreters from him they saw in this course the triumph of Satan, in case they had ever had the slightest faith in the enterprise. Isaac Hale seemed so anxious to break up the marriage and see Emma reinstated in the full fellowship of his household as well as in the Methodist Church, that he was glad to sit in the circle around the cracker barrel in the village grocery store and tell the wide-eyed neighbors the latest developments in connection with the gold plates.

Judging from the affidavits he was glad to furnish such vicious characters as Philastus Hurlburt, we can imagine what gossip and scandal he was anxious to pour into eager ears in the grog shops at Harmony. The repercussions from his oratory were felt when the translation was resumed.

When Oliver Cowdery had come to serve as scribe it was almost as precarious to attempt to translate in Harmony as it had been in Palmyra. They had labored but a short time until Joseph asked Oliver if he knew of some place where they could go to finish the translation. Oliver immediately wrote his dear friend David

Whitmer, again assuring him that this was the work of the Lord and asking if it would be possible for them to enjoy the hospitality of the Whitmer home until the translation was completed. If the Whitmers would make them welcome for a few weeks it was his wish that David would drive down to Harmony and transport them to his father's home in Fayette. When the message was read to the Whitmer family they were anxious to render any assistance that their friend Oliver might petition for. Especially Elizabeth Ann was anxious to see the school master back in their home.

It was agreed that just as soon as David completed some necessary work in the field he would leave at once with a team and wagon to bring Joseph, Emma, and Oliver to his father's home. The next morning when he drove his team to the field to finish plowing a field that contained "between five and seven acres of land" yet to be plowed, he was amazed to find that it had all been plowed during the night, and the plow was left standing where the last furrow had been turned.

While harrowing in a field of wheat he had previously sown by hand he was amazed to discover that he accomplished more in a few hours than he usually did in two or three days. The following day he went to another field to spread some plaster which had previously been dumped in large piles. To his surprise he found that the work had been done exactly as he would have done it himself. His married sister, the wife of Hiram Page, who lived near this field said she saw three men doing the work in his field. She and her husband had observed with what remarkable skill and speed they worked, but did not talk with them.[1]

With this miraculous help in his behalf he was soon convinced, that a power higher than man's was assisting him. This increased his testimony in the favorable reports Oliver had written

---

[1] *Kansas City Journal*, June 5, 1881; *Millennial Star*. XL. 769-774; George Q. Cannon, *Life of Joseph Smith*. p. 67; B. H. Roberts. *New Witnesses for God*. II, 101; Joseph Fielding Smith. *Life of Joseph F Smith*, p 243.

to him. All members of the family concurred in this opinion and were anxious for David to depart at once and bring the two men to the Whitmer home.

A few days later Joseph and Oliver left their work. and walked a short distance up the turnpike where they met David, as Joseph had predicted. The two men climbed into the wagon and greeted the welcome benefactor. Years later David related the circumstances of this meeting in these words:

> That Joseph had informed him (Oliver) when I started from home, where I had stopped the first night, how I read the sign at the tavern; where I stopped the next night, etc.; and that I would be there that day before dinner, and this was why they had come out to meet me: all of which was exactly as Joseph had told Oliver at which I was greatly astonished.

Again his faith in this miraculous movement was confirmed. He was convinced that it was certainly the work of God, as Oliver had assured him. No sacrifice would be too great for him to make for the cause.

A few days later they were at the Whitmer home ready to resume the translation. The angel Moroni had taken charge of the precious records before they departed from Harmony. The danger from the enemy seemed greater than it was in Palmyra when the plates were concealed in a keg of beans as they left that community. Soon after their arrival in Fayette the plates were returned to the translator as they were ready to continue the important labor.

Every precaution was taken at this welcome rendezvous to prevent any interference by the enemy. There must be no demonstration of mob violence, no disharmony, no persecution. This was June, 1829. The plates had been in his. possession since September, 1827. Time was passing rapidly, yet the translated sheets of gold were turning very slowly. This must be their last move. Nothing could be allowed to hinder the work at this tardy hour.

The fact that the Whitmers were all fond of Oliver and perhaps looked forward to his marriage to Elizabeth Ann, was a valuable factor in assuring them the peace and safety they needed for the absorbing labor. Every member of the family must be convinced that this was the work of the Lord. The task of translation must be performed in secrecy. No public meetings would be held for a season and it would not be "noised abroad" that Joseph Smith was in Fayette translating from the gold plates.

The presence of those two men in the Whitmer home for several weeks, so busy with their divine labor that they could not work in the fields, increased the burdens of Mrs. Whitmer, yet no money or labor was offered as recompense. For a time Emma was present to assist with the in, creased household duties, but the men labored through the long hours of the early summer days, scarcely waiting for the scribe to rest his tired hand.

There must be perfect harmony in the home at this time. Though the work of Mrs. Whitmer was greatly increased, she must not become discouraged and send one of her younger sons to call on Willard Chase, George Crane, or other enemies who had done so much in Palmyra to impede the work. There must be perfect unity in the family, every' one knowing that this unpopular cause was absolutely free, from any deception and dishonesty.

As a contributing factor in this direction Joseph gave a sort of patriarchal blessing to three members of the family—David, John, and Peter, Jr.[2] This must have been a source of inspiration and comfort, and assurance that this was surely the work of the Lord.

In that day phrenology was a popular fad. Men traveled throughout the country lecturing on the subject and giving readings. They placed their hands on the head of each person desiring

---

[2] Doctrine and Covenant, Sections 14, 15, and 16.

to have their fortune told, and would attempt to tell their fortune and predict the future by judging solely from the shape of the head.

Let us pause to state that the first mention of the Smith family in the Palmyra newspapers, September, 1824, had reference to this popular fad of phrenology. The enemy had spread abroad the rumor that the Smiths were so poor that they exhumed the body of their son Alvin, who had died the previous year, and sold his head to a phrenologist to be used in his "illustrated lectures." At his own expense the Prophet's father published a denial of this vicious rumor, assuring the public, that he took witnesses with him and the grave was opened and the body had not been disturbed.

People took great delight in having their fortune told by a phrenologist, whose predictions were prompted by his humble knowledge about the contour of the skull and its relation to the shape of the brain. What an inspiration it must have been to the Whitmer brothers to have a man of God place his hands upon their heads or look them in the eye and give a heaven-inspired benediction. Joseph did not measure the skull nor consider the head, he looked into the heart, The many individual revelations given at this time are evidence of the popularity of this type of inspired blessing.

Mrs. Whitmer Sees the Plates

While the Whitmer sons had received a witness and testimony through the translator's inspiring benediction, their mother was given a testimony of this divine work. This account was preserved by the Whitmers, and has been published in many official publications of the Church.[3] This family tradition had made such a lasting impression on David Whitmer that he related it to Orson Pratt

---

[3] *Millennial Star*, XL, 772; Andrew Jenson. *Historical Record*, p. 621; *Doctrine and Covenants Commentary*, p 173; B, H, Roberts, *New Witnesses for God*, II, 105.

and Joseph F. Smith when they interviewed him a short time before his death. He recalled that soon after Joseph and Oliver had resumed the translation in Fayette, his mother was going out to the barn to milk the cows when the angel Moroni appeared to her, explaining to her, "You have been very faithful and diligent in your labors, but you are tired be, cause of the increase in your toil; it is proper, therefore, that you should receive a witness, that your faith may be strengthened." He then showed her the gold plates and no doubt had much to say about them as he called attention to the characters inscribed on the smooth surface of the thin sheets.

We need not reject the account because it was preserved by the Whitmers, most of whom later drifted from the Church, at least for a season. At the dawn of this new movement there was no trained historian or secretary to keep a complete journal of these important events. In 1842 Joseph Smith mentioned another incident which transpired about the same time that Mrs. Whitmer saw the plates. He mentioned, the voice of God in the chamber of old Father Whitmer,"[4] yet this is the only mention ever made in the records of the Church of this important event. The Prophet never commented on it in public and no friend ever interviewed him about it and then recorded the full incident. These two lines are all the information we have on this vital subject.

David explained to his interviewers that the presence of Joseph, Emma, and Oliver in their home greatly increased the toil and anxiety, of his mother. Though she never complained she "had sometimes felt that her labor was too much. This circumstance, however, nerved her up for her increased responsibilities."

It seems perfectly reasonable that any miracle that would preserve the domestic tranquility in the Whitmer home and insure the immediate completion of the translation, was certainly not too

---

[4] Doctrine and Covenants 128:21.

great a price to pay, for such a favor. In the following chapter we shall show how this incident had a direct bearing upon a subsequent revelation.

This was the dawn of the dispensation of the fullness of times. The heavens were again opened and a day of miracles had arrived. Many people were soon to know that this was a "marvelous work and a wonder." The Whitmers received their share of the spirit of the movement and they deserved every blessing they received because of the contribution they made to the cause at that critical time.

Chapter V

THE ELECT LADY

In the spring of 1829 the witnesses were shown the gold plates, The translation was completed in June and the revelation concerning the three special witnesses was given that same month.[1] No doubt Emma was present at the Whitmer home when these miraculous events transpired. It was certainly a test of faith for the two scribes to wait until every page was transcribed before they were permitted to see the plates, yet that was the price they were expected to pay. During the vision a voice declared that "these plates have been translated by the power of God," thus implying that the translation was completed.

While Emma was in Harmony she was daily chided and ridiculed by "Uncle Nat," her father, and other objectors because she was not permitted to see the plates. If they were in her house she should be permitted to see them, it was argued by her assailants. A short time before her death Emma told her sons that the plates were kept in a box under the bed, but she never saw them. Joseph's younger brother, William, once told how disappointed his parents were when the plates were taken to the Smith home, yet they were not allowed to see them. It is perfectly natural that she and other friends would desire to behold the golden volume of scripture.

---

[1] Doctrine and Covenants, Section 17.

Emma had a very jealous disposition. It touched her envious heart painfully when eleven men were shown the plates, but she likely had trouble sleeping for a few nights after Mrs. Whitmer saw the golden record and the angel Moroni. While in Fayette with her husband he comforted her and tried to explain why she should not see the plates. Perhaps he had offered the same advice to his own mother. In the home of the Whitmers, Emma was able to brush aside her tears and become reconciled to this disappointment, but the moment she was back in the Hale tavern where her father and that "powerful local preacher Uncle Nat" kept calling her attention to the fact that the said plates were not in Joseph's possession any more, yet she had never seen them, her jealous heart was filled with bitterness.

"Even the old lady Whitmer saw 'em, but did Emma?" her opponents likely argued. "No, the angel couldn't find her. Old lady Whitmer couldn't get to the cow barn without running into the angel, but where was poor Emma then?"

Knowing the heart of Isaac Hale as it is revealed to the historian, one can hear a barrage of such stupid, yet disturbing questions thundering in Emma's ears for weeks. He and his colleagues were determined to prejudice her against her husband and fill her tender heart with such hatred and disappointment that she would leave him. The strongest weapon they had in their arsenal of arguments was the incident of. the witnesses seeing the plates. They surely used these arguments often and well in an attempt to turn Emma against her husband and the new society that had recently been organized.

Emma had gained a strong testimony while at the Whitmer home. She had seen her husband give blessings to three of the Whitmer sons, upon whom the benediction had made such a profound impression. She shared the religious fervor and sacred spirit that occasioned the showing of the plates to the witnesses; the organization of the Church; the early meetings and baptisms in the new Church, and the reception of several marvelous, revelations. These experiences reinforced her against the "fiery darts of the enemy."[2]

No doubt Emma had much to say to her husband about this subject, at least reminding him of every argument she was forced to listen to every time she saw her antagonists. Her complaints were heard beyond the big bend in the majestic river. They were heard in heaven and the Lord answered.[3] This was the only revelation addressed to Emma Smith. It was a source of comfort and consolation. After it was recorded she was not so easily influenced by the arguments she was forced to listen to from her opponents. This remarkable document was written just a short time before she left Harmony, never to return.

Emma, the Hymn Collector

It must have been a source of inspiration to be given the important assignment of making a selection of sacred hymns to be sung in the meetings of the Saints. She had attended such meetings in Fayette and likely recognized the need for such a collection that would be compatible with the doctrines and spirit of the new society. She had always been active in the Methodist Church in Harmony and realized the contribution sacred music made in any devotional service. Though there are many references in the Bible to the value of music in religious worship, this is the only instance on record where the Lord directed by revelation the compilation of hymns and recognized the contribution they played in worship.

Hymn books were unknown before the time of King James I of England. It was during his reign that the Protestant translation

---

[2] Doctrine and Covenants 28:17.
[3] Doctrine and Covenants, Section 25.

of the Bible issued from the press, bearing the name of that monarch. For years there had been metrical versions of the Psalms and isolated hymns to be found in great numbers, but no regular hymn book was to be found. In 1623, George Wither published his volume of Hymns, and Songs of the Church. From that time forward they became very popular. By 1830 the popular revival movements had made the hymn book as essential in worship as the Bible or the minister.

Doubtless Emma entered into the heaven-inspired assignment immediately, borrowing freely from the Methodist hymn book before she left Harmony, as many songs from that source were included in her compilation. With the passing years she continued, her research, searching among the published hymns or other denominations, her calling was to "make a selection of sacred hymns," not to compose them. She spent much time studying the popular hymns that were sung in other denominations and selected the ones that were appropriate for the Latter-day Saints to sing in their religious services.

When she discovered the talented song writers within the Church she likely encouraged them to contribute to her collection, since W. W. Phelps, Parley P. Pratt, and others were well represented in her collection.

On May 1, 1832, W. W. Phelps was ordered to "correct and print the hymns which have been selected by Emma Smith in fulfillment of the revelation." Many of these hymns were published in the *Evening and Morning Star* during 1832 and 1833, but when the printing press was destroyed by the enemy in July, 1833, much of the manuscript was destroyed. In 1835 it was "decided that Sister Emma Smith proceed to make a selection of sacred hymns according to the revelation and that President W. W. Phelps be appointed to revise and arrange them for printing."

These two were busy again at their important labor. Brother Phelps composed twenty nine hymns that were included in her collection. She freely gleaned from the published hymn books that were available, songs by Isaac Watts, the Wesley brothers, Dr. Rippon, Samuel Medley, Bishop Ken, Newton, Keene, Fellows, and others. Other contributors within the Church included Eliza R. Snow, Parley P. Pratt, Edward Partridge, Philo Dibble, and Thomas B. Marsh.

In 1835 her first collection was published, containing ninety hymns, many of which appear in the latest hymn books of the Church. In 1840 this volume was revised and published in England, running through twenty five, editions. In 1839 her commission was confirmed and she continued her assignment of collecting hymns. The second edition was published in 1841, a vest-pocket edition containing three hundred forty hymns.

Despite the pressure of home duties, Emma gave the Church a great service in this important labor. After the martyrdom and the exodus from Nauvoo her scrapbook continued to grow thicker with the passing years. One year after her son was made president of the Reorganized Church, that humble organization published a volume of her hymns. In 1864 they printed a larger edition, many of which are still sung in the devotional services of that society.

During all her research she was partial to the hymns of the Methodist Church, which she had sung in her youth under the direction of her "Uncle Nat." The influence of that organization remained with her even after she could go no more "with him at the time of his going." On December 27, 1847 she gave her heart in marriage to Lewis C. Bidamon in the lonely Mansion House in Nauvoo. It was a Methodist minister who performed the ceremony.

The revelation given in Harmony in the summer of 1830,

calling the "elect lady" to select hymns for the Church and encouraging her to support her husband and to cease murmuring because she had not enjoyed the gift of miracles as others had richly received, was the turning point in her eventful life. This was the Magna Carta to her as Section 20 was to the Church. Joseph Smith might have left Harmony alone had this valuable revelation not been given to Emma at that critical time. Her willingness to accept and obey it is a monument to her character.

An Elect Lady

In this precious document she is called "an elect lady," a dignified title that remained with her through her life. She was so pre-eminent in her own right, not merely as the wife of Joseph Smith, that she was soon known as "the elect lady." Twelve years later when she was appointed, president of the Relief Society, her husband commented on this title, explaining that it means "one who is appointed to do a certain work in the Church," and that the promise made in 1830, now had its fulfillment as she assumed the leadership of this organization. In this capacity she was president of a great benevolent society, a pioneer in the field of the emancipation and exaltation of women.

An early paragraph in this historic document cautioned her to "murmur not because of the things which thou hast not seen," explaining that it was wisdom that they be "withheld from thee and from the world." In the life of Emma Smith this was the most important revelation her husband ever received. If the facts were only known we would likely hail this as the inspired epistle that persuaded Emma to remain with her husband and the Church. It was received more than a year after the plates had been shown to the witnesses, showing how that disappointment lingered in her broken heart. Had it not been for this revelation she may have remained in Harmony to keep a lonely vigil over the grave of her son, and return to the Methodist Church and the full fellowship of her, family.

She had been present when revelations were received for Joseph's father and some of his brothers, for. Joseph Knight, the three witnesses, and the Whitmer sons. She was present when that great constitutional document was given the day the Church was organized,[4] realizing the heavenly thrill it was to see good men mentioned in these holy documents. This was the highlight of her, career, a climax to three years of persecution, a reward for every moment of despair and disappointment she had experienced since she cast her lot with the man she loved.

Since her husband's ministry in Harmony would soon be terminated and he would soon be pushing back the western horizons, Emma may have succumbed to the repeated requests of her kinsmen and remained with them it this important message had not been given at this critical time. Emma recognized this as a heaven-inspired epistle when she was advised "to go with him at the time of his going and be a scribe and a comfort unto my servant."

The moment this revelation was read to her she likely held her, head high, her full, round face set as flint, and bravely told all her antagonists that she was now ready to turn her back on the village of Harmony and all it contained that was dear to her, and march shoulder to shoulder with her husband through the troubled years.

At her funeral in 1879, an intimate friend delivered an oration titled "The elect lady... thou shalt go with him at the time of his going." It contained these poignant tributes:

> In her youth he gave her heart and hand to a poor illiterate young man. By this act she invited the displeasure of her family. For a brief season they received her back, then turned

---

[4] Doctrine and Covenants, Section 20.

from her again, and she accompanied her husband to the western wilds. They resided for a season in Ohio, then farther west we see her standing side by side with her companion while surrounded by a hostile foe. Again we behold her, as in tears and bitter anguish she sees her husband torn from her by a ruthless mob and dragged away to prison and prospective death. She is left in poverty and distress, and being no longer able to remain near her husband because of the cruel edict of an inhuman executive, she turns her face eastward and with her little children faces the pitiless winter storm. On foot she crosses the ice of the Father of Waters, her two younger children in her arms, the other two clinging to her dress. Then in anguish and suspense she awaits tidings from her husband, whom she has left in a dungeon surrounded by cruel foes. If in all this she ever murmured or faltered in her devotion re know it not.

At length he joins her and a brief season of repose is granted them, during which she sees her husband rise to eminence and distinction, and she, as she was commanded, delights in the glory that came upon him. But, alas! this is only the calm before the storm. Again the heavy, cruel hand of persecution is upon them and upon a calm summer day they bear to her home the mutilated body of her murdered husband. Thousands pass the bier, and look for the last time on the face of the honored dead. Then she gathers her children around that silent form, and looks upon those calm lips which had in time of trouble pronounced those words so, full of pathos and love, "My beloved Emma choice of my heart. . . . . Again she is here, even in the seventh trouble-undaunted firm, and unwavering-unchangeable, affectionate Emma," and from her full heart cries, "My husband. Oh! my husband; have they taken you from me, at last!" Shall this noble women, this faithful wife, this loving mother, this devoted and humble saint, be denied an honorable mention in history, especially since an effort has been made by the vile traducer of the pure and the good to tarnish her fair name? Not while a sense of justice wields the pen, or there remains in the human breast a love for the good and the brave. Was it not her loving hand, her consoling and comforting words, her unswerving integrity, fidelity, and devotions, her wise counsel, that assisted to make this latter-day work a success? If God raised up a Joseph as a prophet and a restorer of gospel truth, then did he raise up an Emma as an help meet for him.

Noble woman! Rest in peace! When you meet your traducers at the bar of God, justice will be triumphant. Then if not till then, will your virtuous name be honored and proper credit be given for your unselfish sacrifice and your labor of love.

Her granddaughter, the talented Vida B. Smith, paid this tribute to the woman who had the courage to turn her back upon her father's household and "go at the time of his going" with the man she loved:

> From the harvest of long years you came
> With your white-flamed soul and honored name;
> When the time was near you leaned to catch the call
> Where in a land of freedom sweet peace lay over all.
> Long generations, brave from years of old,
> Had brought their glory for your women-mold;
> And in it, lo, the Master-hand had set a spirit flame,
> For He, alone, knew all of why you came.
> He knew why this incarnate something fair;
> Knew what wonder-things it would with spirit share.
> And so He made the heart all warm and soft and sweet—
> A heart for all life's loving truly meet;
> But in the will put iron, that kept the soul

The Elect Lady

In dignified and stateliest control!

For this you came: to meet that other one, and stand
Throughout his life a vibrant shield at hand!
The hand that wove the fabric of the gospel plan
Was under yours; each thread he threw
You watched, to see that it fell true.
The pattern lay before his eye,
You saw the racing shuttle fly,
And checked or hastened, 'til the day
When cold and still the weaver lay.

And when the son took up the plan,
Again you stood to guide the man;
Tall, Gracious, straight, with wondrous eyes,
You kept your counsel kind and wise;
And your undying trust kept true
To all you loved, and hoped, and knew.

For this you came,—a high estate,
To keep the heart's wild beating straight;
To guard the spirit, hold the soul
Calm and serene while storms should roll
And thunders break, and friends betray—
A blest, high-tower of strength to stay.
Today we stand, with great desire
To light our torch by that same fire;
To keep our watch, to hold control,
Yet give, of consecrated soul.

We bring an offering to you
And consecrate ourselves anew
To unreserved service wise,
Wherever need for service cries;
As true as you,

> As brave, sweet, grave,
> Calm and serene, as you have been,
> To meet the storm with heart as warm,
> With gentile will, speak or be still,
> To say "I must," and keep each trust,
>
> In memory, brave one, of thee—
> Our Elect Lady!

At the time of her death the newspaper in Nauvoo carried a long article about her. We quote these paragraphs:

> After the services were over, the large company filed through the room past the coffin, viewing the face of the deceased as they passed. It was a touching sight to see those citizens so long acquainted with the silent sleeper, while she was living, pausing beside her to take a last look at her peaceful face, so calm amid the grief of the assembly. Now and then one to whom she had been dearer than to .others would caress the extended hand, or gently stooping lay a hand upon the cold face or forehead, some even kissing the pale cheek in an impulse of love and regret. But scenes of grief must pass- the family at length took leave of her whom they had so long known and loved. The coffin lid was put in place. The six bearers, raised their burden reverently, and with the mourning train, passed to the place of interment upon the premises of her eldest son, near by, where with solemn hymn and fervent prayer the remains were left to their long repose.
>
> The assembly was large; almost everyone knew Mrs. Bidamon some intimately and for many years; some but for a few months, but it is safe to say that the respect, esteem, and love with which she was regarded by all is but a just tribute to the sterling virtues of the woman, wife, and mother, whom the community so soberly, so sadly, and so tenderly

laid away to rest, on that beautiful May day, by the side of the Father of Waters, the mighty Mississippi.

Years later her eldest son wrote these lines as a tribute to her memory:

> I miss thee, my mother: thine image is still
>   The deepest impressed on my heart;
> And that tablet, so faithful, in death shall be chill
>   E'er a line of that image depart.
> Thou Wert torn from my side when I treasured thee most,
>   When my reason could measure thy worth—
> When I knew, but too well, that the idol I'd lost
>   Could ne'er be replaced upon earth.
>
> I miss thee, my mother, when young health hath fled
>   And I sink in the languor of pain:
> Where, where is the arm that once pillowed my head
>   And the ear that once heard me complain?
> Other hands my caress: gentle accents may fall,
>   For the fond and the true are yet mine,
> I've a blessing for each, I am grateful to all;
>   But whose care can be soothing as thine?
>
> I miss thee, my mother, oh, when do I not?
>   Though I know 'twas the wisdom of heaven
> That the deepest shade fell on the sunniest spot,
>   And such is o devotion were riven,
> For when thou wert with me, my soul was below;
>   I was chained to the earth I then. trod;
> My thoughts, my affections, were earthbound, but now
>   They have followed thy spirit to God.

Chapter VI

THRUSTING IN THE SICKLE

It was a great relief to the translator and his scribe when the translation was completed and they were free to launch the public ministry of the Church. For weeks they had devoted their full time to the task of translation. It was a welcome relief when they were free to devote their time and attention to other matters-holding meetings, answering questions about the Book of Mormon, receiving revelations, and other sacred duties that awaited their attention.

Martin Harris the Penitent

For months Martin had been obsessed with a strong desire to see the gold plates. Because of the opposition in his own home he sought such a favor perhaps more than any other person. In the first revelation given to him concerning this subject he was advised to humble himself in mighty prayer and faith," and he would eventually be permitted to "view the things which he desired to see."[1]

After losing the manuscript he had copied and being severely rebuked for the same,[2] he tried to humble himself and be reinstat-

---

[1] Doctrine and Covenants, Section 4.
[2] Doctrine and Covenants, Section 10.

ed in Joseph's good graces. He sought every occasion to be of service at that time of crisis, hoping that he might yet see the golden plates. It was a time of rejoicing when he was informed by revelation that if he would humble himself he should be shown "the plates, and also the breastplate, the sword of Laban, and the Urim and Thummim."[3]

After the angel appeared to the three special witnesses and exhibited the sacred relics of the Nephites, it is perfectly natural that Martin would sign a contract agreeing to pay for the publication of the Book of Mormon. In a subsequent revelation given a few days before the Church was organized, he was advised to "pay the debt thou has contracted with the printer."[4] To obey this command he was obliged to sell a large parcel of his estate. His wife was so thoroughly disgusted with her husband's "credulity" that she secured a divorce and was given eighty acres of land "one of the best in town," as a financial settlement.

Martin sold one hundred fifty acres of his remaining farm to pay the printer. Obliged to sell at that inopportune time he received only $20.00 an acre for that choice property. This price included the crop of wheat that Martin had sown.

The Book of Mormon did not sell in New York. It required seven years to sell the Palmyra edition. There is no record that much of the money was ever returned to the prosperous farmer who had lost his estate and his wife in order to raise money for the publication f the book. Many copies were sold by missionaries who used the money to defray their personal expenses. At a time when every spare dollar was added to the temple fund in Kirtland, it is very likely that the money received from the sale of this book was added to that fund, very little of it getting back to the man who financed the printing of the book.

One of the oldest letters of Joseph Smith's that has been pre-

---

[3] Doctrine and Covenants, Section 17.
[4] Doctrine and Covenants 19:35.

served was written by him soon after he went to Ohio. It was addressed to Martin Harris, requesting that he hasten to Ohio in the early spring, bringing a wagon load of "the books" with him. At his own expense and with his own team and wagon he was on his way when the roads were open for travel, his wagon stacked high with boxes of "the book."

This historic revelation to Martin was the turning point in his life. It was the inspired message that meant as much to him as the revelation had meant to Emma Smith. This was the document at that time of crisis which gave Martin courage to turn his back on his opponents and hearken unto the word of the Lord. It took great courage to sell most of his estate, give eighty acres to his estranged wife, and walk out of his home, leaving Lucy and their three children. Nothing but that historic document could have given him the courage for such a decision which would cost him so much.

Mrs. Harris later said in an affidavit that Martin's estate was worth $10,000 before he paid for printing the Book of Mormon. "He is now an object of pity," she assured her interviewers.[5] If Martin had remained valiant in the Church he would never have become an object of pity. His future course shows what happens to one who becomes delinquent. As we consider the later life of this vacillating man we can read with greater meaning the revelations that were given to him at an early day, all of which cautioned and warned him of a miserable future unless he became more faithful and valiant.

At this point we must say a few words about his family that later came to Utah, which was his second family, not the one he left in Palmyra. In Kirtland he married Caroline Young, the daughter of Brigham Young's brother John. Her mother was Theodocia Kimball. Caroline was stricken with smallpox as a

---

5 J. H. Hunt, *History of the Mormons*, p. 64.

young woman, leaving her beautiful face scarred so badly that she resolved never to marry, but she could not resist the proposal of Martin Harris. He was thirty-three years older than his bride. Five children were born to this union, all of them being born in Kirtland except the last one, who was born in Iowa in 1856.

It is probable that the vacillating Martin had changed his mind again and was headed for Beaver Island in Lake Michigan where the apostate James J. Strang had established his "kingdom." His second wife had remained faithful to him through the years, providing for the little family in Kirtland while her husband was in England as a missionary for Strang, but she was determined to go to Utah and associate with her kindred if she had to go without him. There was a parting of the way soon after their last child was born, as she left him, took her children and made the long journey to Utah, while Martin soon returned to Kirtland after the death of Strang.

In Utah, Caroline married John C. Davis in 1860, becoming, an active member in the Church. She passed away in 1888, thirteen years after the death of her first husband. Though Martin returned to the Church in 1870, being baptized by Edward Stevenson at that time, when he received his endowments he gave as his baptism date, April 6, 1830.

When Martin was commanded in 1830 to pay the debt he had contracted with the printer, he was the only person intimately associated with the rise of Mormonism who could raise the money for such an enterprise. The Smiths had worked hard to pay for their homestead and be free from debt, but when the last payment fell due in the early summer they were unable to raise the money until after harvest time, so some "land sharks" paid the final, payment and took possession of the farm. Joseph Smith, Sr., was put in a debtor's prison for a season and the family was soon obliged to leave the farm they had labored hard to redeem. They moved to Waterloo, not far from Fayette.

This was a hard working family, but they had experienced many financial reverses in New York and Vermont. Joseph's mother was very adept at needlework, often selling many choice samples of her artistic work at the county fairs, bazaars, and other places. His father and brothers were adept at carpentry work, digging wells, making. brooms, boxes, barrels, and other articles that were in demand on the frontier. They made a small push cart which they loaded with sandwiches, cakes, cookies, root beer, and other delicacies, offering them for sale in the village on festive occasions. The boys trapped the fur bearing animals that abounded in the streams and forest, selling their pelts in the village. They sawed and chopped kindling wood, hauling it wherever there was sale for it. Despite these efforts they lost their homestead before they could borrow the final payment from Joseph Knight or other friends.

The Public Ministry of the Church

When the translation was completed and the witnesses had been shown the plates, the sacred records were returned to the angel Moroni. The conclusion is forced upon the historian that the Urim and Thummim were returned with the plates. Joseph had found a seerstone by means of which he could get inspiration much as he did through the sacred stones he found with the gold plates. He retained the seer-stone, but he surely gave the Urim and Thummim back to the angel. That instrument belonged with the plates and he had no more right to keep that instrument than he did to retain the small plates of Nephi. There are a few references in history to the Urim and Thummin which Joseph retained, but the term was used incorrectly. On such occasions they had reference to the seerstone.

The translation finished, they were free to launch the public ministry of the new society. They resumed their preaching and conversation. The great constitutional law of the Church was revealed early in April,[6] and the Church was organized on the sixth day of that month. Such a momentous event would have been held in the Smith home near Palmyra, but the Smiths had lost their property and were living in a small log house in Waterloo. The Whitmer home was much larger and better furnished, so it was offered for that historic meeting.

The Church was organized on Tuesday. The following Sunday a public meeting was held in the Whitmer home and Oliver Cowdery preached the first public discourse in the new organization. In a short time many converts were baptized and the work had commenced to spread. The Book of Mormon came from the press the last week in March, 1830. It was on sale for. one week before the Church was organized.

The Book of Mormon off the press and the new society officially launched, Joseph was free to carry the message to his friends in Broome County. He was especially interested in the Knight family who lived in the "wilderness" country along the Susquehanna about thirty miles. above Harmony. Before Joseph commenced his ministry in the community where the Knights resided, two revelations had been given to Joseph Knight,[7] thus paving the way for a successful ministry in his own family.

Though Joseph and his assistants were untrained for the important labor they: were to perform, it is amazing what a vast array of early documents and historical, material has been preserved. As soon as the Church was organized they were instructed to "keep a record" of all their proceedings. John Whitmer was

---

[6] Doctrine and Covenants, Section 20.
[7] Doctrine and Covenants, Sections 12 and 23.

soon appointed the historian. The humble historical accounts he preserved were retained by him a few years later when he apostatized. His history fell into the hands of the Reorganized Church. In the archives in Salt Lake City, Utah, however, a typed copy of this first historical document is preserved. This same revelation designated Joseph Smith as a "prophet, seer, and translator."

The Baptist Church and other denominations practicing immersion had many members in western New York. When the Whitmers and others were received into the Church by baptism the question arose whether it was necessary to be immersed again after they had previously entered another church by the gateway of immersion. A revelation cleared up this mystery for all time.[8] No revelation was ever given until the Prophet was eagerly awaiting instructions on that particular subject. He was always ripe for learning; always seeking, knocking, asking before revelations were received. They were never thrust upon him, abstract, foreign, unrelated documents, but always came in answer to prayerful meditation.

As soon as the Church was organized many disciples were seeking, the will of the Lord concerning them. One revelation is preserved which was addressed to a group of brethren who had previously had revelations given in their behalf.[9] Such a message reconfirmed their former convictions and fired them with a zeal for the ministry.

The Public Ministry Abroad

Perhaps the young "prophet, seer, and translator" returned with Joseph Knight to his home in Colesville, as he was busy in that village soon after the Church was organized. This was a promising and fruitful field of labor, "white for the harvest." Joseph Knight

---

[8] Doctrine and Covenant, Section 22.
[9] Doctrine and Covenants, Section 23.

had long been a loyal friend to the Smiths. They intended getting a loan from him to make the final payment on their farm, but he lived one hundred miles away and they were Unable to make that journey before the payment had been made by the "land sharks" who soon took possession, of the property. This good friend was at the Smith home when Joseph received the plates, and again when the Church was organized.

The Knights seemed better prospects than the Hales and others who were so perfectly contented and satisfied with their own denominations. The Knights were Universalists, liberal, broad minded, and sympathetic. They made the young prophet welcome in their home and invited their neighbors to attend the cottage meetings and hearken to his words.

Many meetings were held in that community and a few converts were soon made. With the Knights expressing belief in the new doctrines they had great influence with their friends, many of whom soon came into the Church. As the Gospel seeds took root in the hearts of the disciples in Colesville, the enemy became determined to drive the missionaries from the community and put an end to the work. Before he was obligated to flee from Colesville he had made a lasting impression on many people. The first miracle in the Church was performed in that village-casting the evil spirit from Newel Knight.

Soon after Joseph returned to Waterloo he was followed by Newel Knight who had gained a testimony and insisted on being baptized. He was baptized by David Whitmer. After a short visit in Fayette, Joseph was back in Colesville, perhaps returning with the new disciple as he hastened homeward to tell the good news to others. Emma and Oliver were with him and for several days they held many meetings and visited with the friends who were interested, and laid the foundations for a thriving branch in that area.

At one baptismal service they baptized thirteen persons, including Emma Smith and the wife of Newel Knight. It would have been an occasion of remorse and embarrassment t her family if Emma had been baptized at a public service in Harmony. She was wise in receiving this ordinance away from home. Joseph Knight heeded the advice he had received by revelation,[10] and was baptized at that time.

Since the Knights were respectable citizens, highly respected in the community, their course had a powerful influence on others who were not afraid to listen to the missionaries and consider their words with prayerful attention.

When the enemy waged a bitter persecution against these missionaries they left Colesville and hastened southward to Harmony. It was in this same "wilderness" country between these two little villages that the keys of the higher priesthood were restored by Peter, James, and John one year before.[11] They had been arrested twice in Colesville and subjected to great abuse and embarrassment. It was a relief to get away for a season from the enemies in Broome County, though other enemies awaited them wherever they went.

Disharmony Along the Susquehanna

Back in Harmony the days were hardly long enough for them to accomplish the many duties they wished to perform. The enemy at that place had heard of the strange miracle at the Knight home and the persecution that had followed their work in that community. The same Satanic spirit was soon to be overcome in Harmony.

The divinely-established Church had been organized; the heavens opened; the gift of seership, prophecy, revelation, and

---

[10] Doctrine and Covenants 23:7.
[11] Doctrine and Covenants, Sections 27, and 128:20-21.

translation again upon the earth. Endowed with these divine gifts there was much work to be done to lay the firm foundations of the new society that would soon spread to all the civilized nations of the earth. In fact the ministry at that time was so replete with miraculous events that these busy men did not make a complete record of all the marvelous events, miracles, and revelations that were enjoyed at that time.

An epistle written by the Prophet in 1842 made a brief reference to some of these incidents that are not fully explained elsewhere. We must consider two paragraphs from this famous document, bearing directly on the places and incidents now under consideration:

> And again, what do we hear?... The voice of Michael on the banks of the Susquehanna, detecting the devil when he appeared as an angel of light! The voice of Peter, James, and John in the wilderness between Harmony... and Colesville...And again the voice of God in the chamber of old Father Whitmer.[12]

Our limited history at that early period, however, has preserved enough documents to show what a busy career the young reformer had during the last few weeks he spent in Harmony. He planned on neglecting the ministry for a season in order to plow and plant and till the soil, having purchased thirteen acres of land from his father-in-law. The deed is still on record which transferred this property to Joseph Smith in the early summer of 1830. The young seer expected to labor with his own hands for his support, as certain prophets among the Nephites had done. For this reason he hastened to Harmony soon after the Church was organized, the Book of Mormon off the press, and a branch established in Colesville.

Oliver had returned to Harmony with him to assist in the

---

[12] Doctrine and Covenants 128:20-21.

temporal labor in his small field, completing the planting as soon as possible o they could devote their time to the ministry. The first revelation they received after returning to the small parcel of land to put in a crop and labor with their own hands for their support, called them from the field and the furrow to a more important labor, the ministry. They were enjoined to "magnify thine office; and after thou hast sowed thy fields and secured them, go speedily unto the church which is in Colesville, Fayette, and Manchester, and they shall support thee; and I will bless them both spiritually and temporally."[13]

If this admonition had not been given by revelation the ministry would have been sadly neglected for a time, The young prophet was so modest and humble that he would have been reluctant to ask his friends for financial support unless he had a revelation in manuscript form to show them. This admonition magnified the office he had assumed and cheapened the drudgery of tiling the soil, sowing, cultivating, harvesting. This holy message reminded him of another harvest he had often been told about-the important harvest of souls. He must now put aside the hoe and the shovel and go out in the full majesty of his divine office and labor with his might in the human field that was white, already to harvest.[14]

Though these two missionaries labored in the field during the clay time they were free at night to meditate upon the things of the kingdom and plan for the future. During the few weeks that they spent laboring in the field they did not forsake the ministry or fail to keep in tune with the spirit that directed the work. It was at this time that another revelation was given, the one that called Emma to the task of selecting hymns and advising her not to murmur because the gifts of the spirit had not been poured out upon her as others had received them. At this time when the trials and

---

[13] Doctrine and Covenants 24:3.
[14] Doctrine and Covenants 4:4.

persecutions at Colesville were so fresh in their memory and the same spirit was manifest in Harmony, she was advised to be "a comfort unto my servant . . . in his afflictions with consoling words, in the spirit of meekness." She had heard so many vicious things said against him that she may have been reluctant to defend and comfort him with consoling words.

Now that the humble crops were planted and Joseph was about ready to depart from Harmony, never to return, she was wisely advised "to go with him at the time of his going."[15] In the midst of the Satanic opposition that abounded in that locality these two valuable revelations were given. We cannot over estimate the intrinsic value of these two great documents. Without the latter, Emma may have remained at Harmony, returning to the fold of the Methodist Church and the good graces of her family. Without the former, Joseph would have neglected the ministry to labor in the furrow and the field, and the forest so his sensitive heart would not need to beg for bread.

At this time and subsequently much information was revealed concerning the "Words of Moses." A discussion of this subject will be reserved for a later chapter, but it was at this time that the first part of that great document was revealed. It was to serve as a preface to the book of Genesis in the inspired study of the scriptures he was advised to commence soon after the Book of Mormon was printed.

In July the historian John Whitmer was visiting in Harmony for a few days. A revelation was received at that time advising them to devote their time "to the studying of the scriptures, and to preaching, and to confirming the church at Colesville, and to perform your labors on the land. such as is required, until after you shall go to the west to hold the next conference; and then it shall be made known what you shall do."[16]

---

[15] Doctrine and Covenants 25:4-6.
[16] Doctrine and Covenants 26:1.

This had reference to the conference that was to be held in Fayette the following September, at which time he was on the threshold of a great career farther to the west.

Instructions on the Sacrament

At the last baptismal service in Colesville the missionaries were obliged to flee in haste without confirming several of the new converts, including Emma Smith and the wife of Newel Knight. Early in August, Newel Knight and his wife visited the missionaries in Harmony, perhaps taking many provisions and supplies to them. It was decided that a confirmation meeting would be held in the humble hut back of the Hale tavern. Since Joseph had no wine in the house he set out to purchase some from a neighbor. In the orchard a short distance from the house an angel appeared to him, explaining that it was not necessary to use wine for sacramental purposes, "if it so be that ye do it with an eye single to my glory."[17]

Aware of the many enemies in the village who might add poison to any wine these men purchased, they were further advised not to "purchase wine, neither strong drink, of your enemies. Wherefore, you shall partake of none except it is made new among you." These men had never seen water used for sacramental purposes and were reluctant to substitute it in this service. They "prepared" wine of their own make for this meeting, perhaps picking some green grapes and crushing the sour juice from them.

In many churches the sacramental wine has been diluted with water, but to replace it entirely with water was a new and daring procedure. One minister objected to such a substitution in these bold words:

> Whosoever puts away true and real wine, or fermented grape

---

[17] Doctrine and Covenants 27:2.

juice, on moral grounds, from the Lord's Supper, sets himself up as more moral than the Son of God who reigns over his conscience, and than the Savior of souls who redeemed him. There has been absolutely universal consent on this subject in the Christian Church until modern times, when the practice has been opposed, but solely on prudential considerations.[18]

The revelation authorizing this substitution was the last recorded revelation given in Harmony. In fact the latter part of Section 27 was given after they had returned to Fayette.

Newel Knight, his wife, and their children shared the hardships of the Saints in New York, Ohio, Missouri, and Illinois They were with the caravans that rolled across the Iowa prairies when the exodus was in progress. When they reached the Missouri they cast their lot with the recalcitrant, Alpheus Cutler, who took a small colony northward into the Indian territory. Newel Knight died in that temporary rendezvous January 11, 1847. His widow and children made their way to the Salt Lake Valley in 1850.

After Joseph had "sown his fields and secured them" he was ready to pull up stakes and magnify his office. He never came back to harvest his crops or sell his possessions. The ministry could not be neglected for such paltry trifles.

Peter Ingersoll of Manchester later testified in an affidavit that he was hired to drive down to Harmony in August, 1830, and transport Joseph and his friends to Fayette. He related that when they were ready to mount the loaded wagon and follow the Susquehanna through the beautiful rolling "wilderness" country, Isaac Hale, heart-broken because Emma had not been persuaded to remain with him, uttered his final benediction with a "flood of tears," in these words, "You have stolen my daughter and married her. I had rather have followed her to her grave."[19]

---

[18] A. A. Hodge, *Popular Lectures on Theological Themes*, p. 400.
[19] E. D. Howe, *Mormonism Unveiled*, p. 234.

These words reveal the bitter heart of Isaac Hale and magnify the importance of the revelation that designated Emma as "an elect lady" and encouraged her "to go with him at the time of his going."[20]

As the heavy wagon lumbered out of the yard, past the stump mortar where the meal had been ground for the family, there were tears in Emma's eyes as she looked back at her weeping parents, brothers, and sisters who refused to wave a final farewell as Emma waved her hand as a token of friendly departure. From that moment she never saw her parents again. She was riding out of their lives forever, a painful experience she may have never been able to do without the strength that came to her through the revelation her husband had received in her behalf.

When Lot's family made such an exodus from the cities on the plain, they were commanded not to look back but Emma doubtless watched the old homestead as long as it could be seen as they followed the beautiful stream northward. There were tears in her, eyes and a lump in her throat as she cast a final glance at the mound of earth beneath which slept her infant son. Many unkind words have been spoken against Emma Smith and the course she pursued after the death of her husband, but we must pay her a great tribute at this early time. Only a bold, courageous woman deeply in love with her husband could make such a sacrifice and pay the price Emma was willing to pay for fellowship in the humble, unpopular society for which her husband was destined to write his testimony with his own blood.

The Colesville Saints Go West

Joseph and Oliver had been in Harmony but a short time until Joseph Knight called on them, inviting them to return with him and preach to the people in that community, many of whom

---

[20] Doctrine and Covenants 25:6.

seemed very interested in the new society. They returned with him, and were soon building up a strong branch in that area. When the Saints were commanded to push westward the members at Colesville were among the first to make that exodus.[21]

The disciples from Colesville having been united by a common bond, having been subject to abuse and persecution from the moment they made Joseph Smith welcome in their homes, remained together as an integrated group for many years. Down through the years they are known as the Colesville branch.[22] Subsequent revelations mentioned this integrated group or its individual members.[23]

A few years later a member of this branch, a sister of Newel Knight's wife, having joined the Church for a season and then apostatized, has left a first hand account of conditions in Colesville. We quote the following pages from her book:

> Two years had elapsed; at this time my sister had married and lived in the town of Colesville, Broom County, New York. Her husband's name was Newell Knight. He was a staunch Universalist, and his father, Joseph Knight, was also of the same belief. Sister Sarah was of the Presbyterian faith. However, I never knew of any argument between them concerning their religious views. I was now just entering my third year at my brother's and a revival of religion commenced in the Presbyterian church, and many were exhibiting a great interest in forming a new and more useful life; and I found myself one of that happy number.
>
> During this revival, many were brought to see that the blood of Christ was sufficient to cleanse them from all sin; and I felt an assurance that I was also adopted into the family of God, through his blood. I was now, as I considered—and in fact it

---

[21] Doctrine and Covenants 38:32.
[22] Joseph Fielding Smith, Essentials in Church History, pp. 120, 127, 129.
[23] Doctrine and Covenants, Sections 37, 51, and 54.

was my most earnest wish-to lay aside selfish longings, and look a little to the comfort and good of others. It is true I now had, at an early age, learned a trade; and choosing not to eat the bread of idleness, and furthermore to let independence be my aim, and ever look upon avarice as my worst foe, I felt determined to start out in the right path in pursuing the journey of life. To emulate the example of the good Samaritan effectually, no one must be in possession of an independence....

Six months had elapsed, and we hear a rumor going around that Joe Smith, of whom we had often heard as a fortune teller, was at this time in Colesville, preaching a very strange doctrine, and that our sister and her husband were attentive listeners to his fanaticism. This rumor staggered our wits to comprehend. The story was repeated in our ears almost daily. We knew this same Joe Smith had often been in Colesville, to visit his Universalist friends or brethren. I had seen him two or three times, while visiting at my sisters, but did not think it worth my while to take any notice of him. I never spoke to him, for he was a total stranger to me. However, I thought him odd looking and queer. He also told his friends that he could see money in pots, under the ground. He pretended to foretell people's future destiny, and, according to his prognostication, his friends agreed to suspend their avocation and dig for the treasures, which were hidden in the earth; a great share of which, he said, was on Joseph Knight's farm.

Old Uncle Joe, as we called him, was a wool carder, and a farmer; yet he abandoned all business, and joined with a number of others, to dig for money on his premises....

I now visited my sister to try if possible to convince her of the error into which she had innocently been decoyed and deceived. However, this was of no effect whatever. She was as firm as the everlasting hills in the belief of Mormonism, and seemed to have the whole Bible at her tongue's end. She was of the belief that God had again visited His people, and again set His hand, the second time, to recover the house of Israel. She also was of the belief that this was the work, and warned me against condemning that which I did not understand, lest I should be found fighting against God's will.

By this time my faith had grown weak in regard to changing her mind, and I thought it best for me to go back to my brother's, and henceforth to let them alone. I considered it a deception and delusion; but as I was necessarily detained over the sabbath, I attended services with my sister. The discourse was delivered by Oliver Cowdry, an elder of the Mormon Church, and a witness to the gold plates. After preaching, several were baptized, and the converts were increasing rapidly. For some time, having meetings daily, and also evening, the excitement was great, in so much that many were overcome by the spirit, and were, seemingly, unconscious of all around them. On awakening from this trance, they would say they were happy, and had seen angels and talked with them. However, I did not feel interested in this direction. It had hitherto appeared most simple of all things, and I was decidedly against such proceedings. I was still detained at my sister's. For some reason I could not get back to my brother's, in Sandford; and, at this time, I cannot remember the cause of my prolonged stay. While I tarried I attended church with my sister. Sidney Rigdon came into Colesville and preached to a numerous congregation. We did not class him as a Mormon, as we were informed that he was a Baptist minister, from Painsville, Ohio. The words of his text—"O, foolish Galatians, who hath bewitched you that ye should not obey the truth?" It was indeed interesting, and great attention and silence prevailed; and it was acknowledged by all to be the best sermon ever preached in that vicinity. He stayed several days, seeming to have special business with Joseph Smith and the leaders of the new Mormon church. I mention these facts only because I think to this day that he had something to do in getting up the Book of Mormon, and we found, after his return to Ohio, that he was also a believer in the new doctrine.

This seemed rather strange, that a man of his talents should be a believer in anything so strange as this appeared to be; and, as I was now about to go back to my brother's in Sandford, my sister told me that God would give me a sure witness to the truth of this work, if I would only ask him; it was my custom to daily go to him. I therefore thought to make this an item to be remembered, and, in my feeble petition I humbly asked him to show me the truth of this, least I should be found to rebel against His holy will....

Several had assembled at Newell Knight's, as was the general custom, for he was an elder. A message was sent to me that Esck Lyon wished to see me at the grove, which was some distance from the house: that he wished a friendly interview with me. I felt reluctant in granting his request, but through the advice of my sister I ventured to go. I at this time attempted to make plain to him the reason of my tarrying at my sister's and I then believed he understood me perfectly. While in the midst of our conversation, who should come but the Rev. Mr. Shere, pastor of our church in Sandford....

Not long after this it was circulated that I intended to go into the Mormon church, and a copy of the complaint which was entered against me to the church in Sandford, was handed me. It read as follows:

"To the Church of Christ, in Sandford:

WHEREAS, B. M., a member of said church, embraces a most wicked and dangerous heresy; and whereas, we have taken with her the first and second steps of gospel labor, without obtaining satisfaction, we therefore make complaint to the church of which said B. M. is a member, praying that the brethren of said church would bring her to an account for her unchristian conduct; and as in duty bound, your servants will ever pray.

> H. M.
> E. L.
> B.S."

Now, as time advanced, the little church from Colesville received word from those commissioners who were sent by the church to Missouri to look out lands, and, as preparation had already been made for the journey, we all started for the Ohio river in wagons-twenty-four in number, twelve in each company. The company I was in was called Newell Knight's, and we started one day in advance of the others, as provisions could be more readily purchased for twelve teams than for twenty-four. People all along the road stared at us as they would at a circus or a caravan, and our appearance did not deceive the public eye. We most truly were a band of pilgrims, started out to seek a better country. [24]

The Prophet's Last Days in New York

In September Joseph was back in Fayette. He had built up a thriving branch in Colesville, but the little flock in western New York was in an uproar. Oliver had returned to the Whitmer home a few weeks in advance and had been influenced by the spurious revelations that Hiram Page had been receiving through a "peepstone" he had found. By means of this stone the adversary was trying to undermine Joseph Smith and turn his disciples against him.

---

[24] Einily M, Austin, *Mormonism*, pp. 30, 32, 36, 38, 40, 63.

The Whitmers had been unfavorably influenced by these counterfeit messages. In their presence Oliver soon partook of that negative spirit and found himself opposing his leader. The sinister spirit in Fayette gave Oliver the courage to write to Joseph, insisting that he remove a few lines from the revelation now known as Section 20. The text he objected to was this, "And truly manifest by their works that they have received the Spirit of Christ unto the remission of their sins." His letter contained this daring request, "I command you in the name of God to erase those words, that no priestcraft be amongst us!"

Such an insulting command touched Joseph's tender heart and pained him bitterly. Such a small society did not need two or three heads. There was a heresy in Fayette that must be put down. Joseph hastened from Harmony to Fayette to put and end to this schism and let the world know who was the Lord's mouthpiece in this new dispensation.

This was a time of crisis when a definite decision must be made and disgruntled members whipped into line with the final voice of authority. The Whitmers were a devoted, united family. In the Church and out of the Church they stood shoulder to shoulder, their family ties being stronger than the bonds of society. Since Hiram Page had married one of the Whitmer girls he was regarded as a member of the family. Hiram had recently found a stone by means of which he was receiving spurious revelations. His kinsmen mistook these counterfeit messages for true revelations from the Lord.

On the heels of Oliver's delinquency, Hiram was receiving messages which had a tendency to turn the Whitmers against Joseph Smith. At least if Hiram and Oliver were to be commanding and ordering Joseph about it would magnify these in-laws in the eyes of the Whitmers and relegate Joseph to a humble, mediocre position that was far beneath the dignified position of the first elder, seer, prophet, translator, and revelator.

At the dawn of this movement there was a wave of persecution thrust upon the virgin Church from every quarter. If they were to become a power in the earth there must be unity within their ranks. They were the salt of the earth, a light on a hill. The world would judge this society by its fruits. On the eve of its organization there must be no serious schism in the Church. This error must be put down at once.

The moment the Prophet came into this negative environment he received a revelation that was designed to put an end to such conflict for all time. The advise in this timely epistle applies to delinquents and self-appointed leaders just as much today as it did in 1830. It was addressed to Oliver, but was aimed at Hiram as well. Oliver must first be put in line then he could be used as an instrument to put Hiram in his place.[25]

The first paragraph made it clear that "no one shall be appointed to receive commandments and revelations in this Church, excepting my servant Joseph Smith, Jr. ... and thou shalt not command him who is at thy head, and at the head of the Church." When the penitent Oliver was reclaimed, he was instructed to "take thy brother Hiram Page, between him and thee alone, and tell him that those things which he hath written from that stone are not of me, and that Satan deceiveth him."

Oliver was in a far better position to influence. Hiram than was Joseph Smith or any other friend. His experiences in the new society had magnified him, in the eyes of the Whitmers until his, advice would be gladly accepted by all members of the family. Much of the blame for the Whitmers' apostasy in the following years should be placed on the shoulders of Oliver. It he had remained valiant, upholding the hands of his leader, keeping

---

[25] Doctrine and Covenants, Section 28.

abreast with the progress of the Church, he could easily have influenced the Whitmers to do likewise, but his delinquency seemed to give them a license to follow his course.

The appointment of Oliver as an ambassador to whip Hiram into line was a master stroke of diplomacy. Joseph was quite a stranger to Hiram. He certainly did not know him as Oliver did, nor could he have influenced him as Oliver could. If he had assumed a dictatorial attitude, taking upon himself the sole responsibility of putting Hiram in his place with the voice of authority and the lash of discipline, Hiram's stubborn heart may have been so offended that he would have rebelled against Joseph's domination, perhaps withdrawing from the Church at that time and influencing his friends to follow him.

During the last week in September a conference was held at Fayette. There were sixty-two members in the Church at that time. Before the congregation much was said about Hiram's "peepstone." He acknowledged his error and promised to be loyal to his leader and cease consulting the stone for guidance. Oliver had apologized for his contrary course and was reinstated in the good graces of his leader.

The Page "peepstone," however, was preserved as a souvenir. It is now in the possession of the Reorganized Church. The writer was permitted to examine it. It is a flat stone about seven inches long, four wide, and one, quarter inch in thickness. It is dark gray in color with waves of brown and purple gracefully interwoven across the surface. A small hole has been drilled through one end of it as if a string had been threaded through it. It is simply impressive enough to make a good paper weight, yet it became a tool through which the adversary at, tempted to stir up strife and create a schism in the Church.

Hiram Page had received spurious information about the

building up of Zion, which was a popular theme with the little flock. As soon as he and Oliver were enjoying the hand of fellowship again, one of the greatest revelations yet received was recorded.[26] It is a doctrinal discourse, filled with impressive information that was certainly the climax to the discussions that had taken place at that time. It contained a wealth of information that would magnify the Prophet in the eyes of the congregation, reconfirming them in the faith, and reassuring them that their leader was a man of God who spoke with authority. This masterful document made the spurious preachments of Page look like a child's composition.

With the exception of Section 20 this is the strongest doctrinal document revealed in New York or Pennsylvania. It was given at a time of crisis when the Church was threatened with serious trouble from within. It speaks with finality on several subjects that were widely discussed at the time, most popular of which was the subject of the end of the world and the Millennium. These were popular themes in all the camp meetings and revivals of the area, at which conflicting opinions were freely expressed.

William Miller and the End of the World

Not far away William Miller was agitating the farmer folk on the frontier with his sermons and writings about the second advent of the Lord and the terrible events that would precede it. The woods of western New York rang with his oratory and many were turned to the. Christian way of life for fear of being caught in the Devil's dragnet when he went forth to gather the tares and burn them. By 1831 he had preached so long and loud on this subject that he announced with finality that the Lord would continue to thresh the nations until April 4, 1843, at which time His glorious second advent would be witnessed by the faithful. Typical of the Miller

---

[26] Doctrine and Covenants, Section 29.

oratory that was being heard at this time, in western New York is the following paragraph which considers some of the subjects that are discussed in Section 29:

> The end of the world is at hand. The evidence flows in from every quarter. The earth is reeling to and fro like a drunkard. ...See the carnivorous fowls fly screaming through the air! See—See these signs! Behold the heavens grow black with clouds; the sun has veiled himself; the moon, pale and forsaken, hangs in the middle air; the hail descends; the seven thunders utter loud their voices; the lightnings send their vivid gleams of sulphurous flames abroad; and the great city of the nations falls to rise no more forever and forever. At this dread moment, look! The clouds have burst asunder; the heavens appear; the great white throne is in sight! He comes! He comes! Behold the Savior comes...
>
> Ten years from now Christ will appear a second time in the clouds of heaven. He will raise up the righteous dead and judge them with the righteous living... The earth will be sacrificed by fire and the wicked and all their works shall be consumed. [27]

For many years William Miller had been one of the most popular preachers at the camp meetings and revivals on the frontier. His name appears so often in the records of the Church that we must pause to say more about him at this point. On April 4, 1843, his popularity began to wane. Though Joseph Smith received many revelations concerning the second coming of the Savior and the events that would precede it, he never announced any dates. He was as indefinite as the Savior was when his disciples asked him to name the hour of his return.

Miller was filled with alibis, a characteristic of false prophets. Early in April he was explaining that "When the year 1843 is men-

---

[27] Carl Carmer, *Listen for a Lonesome Drum*, p. 134,

tioned, the Jewish year is intended." Later he admitted that "We do not pretend to be infallible, or not liable to be mistaken a few months, or a few years." Nothing like this was ever done by Joseph Smith. A study of William Miller and his false predictions makes one appreciate the true revelations that were received by the true "prophet, seer, and revelator."

Miller postponed the date of the second coming to March 21, 1844. When this date arrived without the Savior, thousands of his disciples, arrayed in white ascension robes, spent the night on hill tops awaiting the expected return of the Lord. This second disappointment was so great that the dejected "prophet" lay as in a trance for four days. He next set the date of the Lord's return in 1847 and again in 1861. By that time most of the ascension robes were worn out and they decided not to name the exact date again. At the present time his followers believe that "millions now living will never die."

In contrast to this type of wisdom the revelations of Joseph Smith stand out as divine epistles. However, Miller was not the only one who erred in this regard. Hippolitus expected the end of the world to come in the year 500 A. D. All Christendom expected it in the year 1000 A. D. The great event was awaited again in 1260, 1600, 1700, 1715, and 1734. In 1783 Mrs. Buchanan in Scotland announced that she was the woman spoken of in the Apocalypse who was clothed in the sun, and that the end of the world was near at hand. As late as 1936 other false "prophets" were expecting the return of the Savior. The Shakers were also convinced that their leader, Ann Lee, was the woman clothed with the sun, and the moon under her feet.

There are many reference to William Miller in the journal of Joseph Smith. On February 12, 1843, he was asked his opinion of Miller, and "preached them quite a sermon that Miller was in want of correct information upon the subject, and that he was not so much to blame as the translators." On the last day of that month he wrote a long article on the subject, closing with these words. "Surely the Lord God will do nothing, but he revealeth his secrets unto his servants the prophets. Therefore, hear this, o earth: The Lord will not come to reign over the righteous in this world in 1843, nor until everything for the Bridegroom is ready."

Just three weeks before Miller's appointed date arrived, some of the leaders of the Church witnessed a miraculous display of splendor in the heavens. Concerning it the prophet said, "As sure as there is a God in heaven... and as sure as he ever spoke by me, so sure will there be a speedy and bloody war; and the broad sword seen this evening is the sure sign thereof." Yet he wisely avoids the common mistake of naming the hour of such calamities.

On the fourth day of April, 1843, he recorded in his diary, "Miller's day of judgment has arrived, but it is too pleasant for false prophets."

Soon after a Chicago newspaper published a long account written by Joseph Smith about the rise of the Church and its teachings, the same paper printed these lines: "Several Millerites have lately been in our city, and they pronounce Mormonism one of the greatest humbugs of the age; and after that Joseph Smith is the great he-goat spoken of in the scriptural prophecies."

The revolutionary teachings announced at the dawn of the restoration stand out as the words of God in contrast to the creeds of men which were to be found in the rituals and catechisms of the Campbellites, the Shakers, the Millerites, and other denominations that were to be encountered on the Western Reserve, and from which many converts would be gleaned.

More Revelations to Individuals

The revelation recorded in Section 29 also mentioned the gathering of mine elect," which prepared the disciples in New York for the call that would soon come to them to migrate to Ohio. This particular revelation stands out as a masterpiece, fitting into its environment and time so perfectly and answering so many questions that were disturbing so many people at that time, that it soon put an end to the threatened schism and became an integrating force that united the little flock as strongly as the Whitmer family was united in a common cause.

Another revelation reminded the Whitmer brothers that Oliver's position was inferior to that of Joseph's.[28] The next revelation was addressed to Thomas B. Marsh who had recently been baptized. "Pray always, lest you enter into temptation and lose your reward," must not have been heeded by the new convert. A few years later he occupied the second position from the top in the Quorum. of the Twelve, the members having been arranged according to their age. David W. Patten was president of the quorum and Brigham Young followed Marsh. When the enemy killed Patten in Missouri, Marsh had an opportunity to succeed to the presidency of the quorum and eventually to the presidency of the Church, but in the meantime he chose to apostatize. Years later he traveled to Utah and united with the Church again. This time he was an old, broken down man, suffering from palsy and otherwise afflicted from a life of dissipation and abuse. In a meeting one Sabbath he listened to a discussion on the subject of apostates and the fruits of their contrary course. He stood before the class for a moment, trembling, pale, withered and said with the voice of experience, "If you want to see the fruits of apostasy look at me!"

The last few months Joseph spent in New York were crowd-

---

[28] Doctrine and Covenants, Section 30.

ed with important items of business. Many friends who came to interview him were confirmed in the faith as revelations were given in their behalf.[29]

It was a time of triumph and achievement when the first organized missionary journey was launched and the four young men set out to take, the "Indians' Bible" to the Indians.[30]

When these missionaries reached Kirtland, Ohio, their message made such a profound impression on certain religious leaders in that community that two of them, Sidney Rigdon and Edward Partridge, made the long journey to Fayette to interview the Prophet. They each received a special revelation after they manifested faith in the new message.[31]

During these busy months the inspired study of the scriptures that had been started in Harmony was resumed in Fayette. The valuable information that was revealed during that initial and intensive study never found a place in the Doctrine and Covenants, but appears in the Pearl of Great Price, Some of this information had been revealed in June, 1830, the balance of it as that historic year drew to a close. Soon after the "Prophecy of Enoch" was revealed, Joseph was advised not to continue the revision of the scriptures until he should remove to Ohio.[32]

The vast wealth of material that had been given since he began the intensive study of the scriptures did much to inspire the disciples and give them implicit faith in their inspired leader. With him in their midst, imparting wisdom to all who sought his advice, and flooding their eager minds with such gems of wisdom as the "Words of Moses," the "Prophecy of Enoch," and the doctrinal revelations that were recorded at that time, it was perfectly natural that no one would listen again to the spurious announcements from Hiram Page. Such gems of inspiration and wisdom exalted

---

[29] Doctrine and Covenants, Sections 33, 34, 35, 36, and 37.
[30] Doctrine and Covenants, Section 28, 30, and 32.
[31] Doctrine and Covenants, Sections 3 and 36.
[32] Doctrine and Covenants, Section 37.

the Prophet and magnified the ministry in the eyes of the little flock until they would delight in contributing to his support that he might be free from the task of harvesting his meager crop and working long days in the fields for his sustenance.

Oliver was so ashamed because of the insulting letter he had written to his leader, that he was delighted, when the call came for him to depart with three friends and carry the new message to the "border of the Lamanites." This historic missionary tour not only opened the portals in Ohio, but it pushed back the horizons and blazed the trail for the beginning of the western migration.

When their leader was commanded to hasten on to Ohio, the entire membership in Colesville and Fayette was ready to follow the moment he should ask them to pull up stakes and push on to the fringe of the frontier. At the close of the year there were about seventy members in the Church. Orrin Porter Rockwell of Manchester and others who were to become pillars of strength in the coming years, had united with the flock and were eager to follow their leader and help break the wilderness in Ohio.

The dawn of the new year found the seer busy dictating revelations, holding a conference, and pushing forward the work of the ministry. The command to go to Ohio was repeated with the assurance that "I will give unto you my law; and there you will be endowed with power from on high."[33]

The two truth-seekers from Kirtland, Sidney Rigdon and Edward Partridge, were so favorably impressed with the young "prophet, seer and revelator" that they remained for weeks in the community feasting upon the things of the kingdom until the latter part of January. They persuaded Joseph and Emma to return with them at that inclement season of the year, the rest of the disciples to follow in the spring.

By that time thirty-nine revelations, now preserved in the

---

[33] Doctrine and Covenants, Sections 38, 39, and 40.

Doctrine and Covenants, had been recorded. Four of them had been given in Manchester, fifteen in Harmony, and twenty in Fayette. This long list did not include the long document that appears in the Pearl of Great Price, which was not one whit behind the greatest of the revelations that were reserved for publication in the first volume of modern scriptures, the Book of Commandments, Moreover, no record was made at the time of the appearance of "Michael on the banks of the Susquehanna, detecting the devil when he appeared as an angel of light! The voice of Peter, James, and John in the wilderness between Harmony and Colesville... the voice of God in the chamber of old Father Whitmer,"[34] and many other items of inspiration and miracle that were not fully recorded in the humble chronicles at that early date. So far as New York and Pennsylvania were concerned the modern volume of scripture was now closed.

In a few weeks time the ministry had become such an important labor that Joseph would not forsake it for a season to hurry down to Harmony to barter his meager crops for necessities or sell his small tract of land for "filthy lucre." The holy ministry beckoned him on to the Western Reserve! Friends were glad to contribute toward his support and see the new movement roll forward. In the coming months hundreds of faithful disciples would join the new society which was soon to become a great power in the earth. The cold months of 1831 found the little flock without their shepherd. He had gone on to greener pastures to prepare a place for them—and what a place it was, with a people prepared and awaiting his coming.

---

[34] Doctrine and Covenants 128:20-21.

PART II

"The Field is White, Ready for the Harvest."

THE OHIO AND MISSOURI PERIOD

Chapter VII

A PEOPLE PREPARED

"You've prayed me here. Now what do you want of me?" The speaker was Joseph Smith, while the surprised listener was Newel K. Whitney. The place was the store of Gilbert and Whitney in Kirtland, Ohio. It was early in February, shortly after he arrived in the village which was soon to become the headquarters of the Church.

Yes, Newel K. Whitney was among the many who had been exercised by the preaching of four missionaries as they tarried in northern Ohio before continuing their journey to the "border of the Lamanites." Joseph and Emma were made welcome in the Whitney home, where they lived for a few months.

The Whitney family was one of the most respectable and influential families in the community. To gain their friendship and be invited to share their hospitality for a few months magnified the favored guests in the eyes of the public. It is said that Joseph had seen the Whitneys in vision praying for his coming to Kirtland.

The Whitneys related that they were once praying fervently to know how they might receive the gift of the Holy Ghost, of which the "Campbellite" missionaries had preached so much, when they beheld a cloud of glory resting upon their house and heard a voice saying, "Prepare to receive the word of the Lord, for it is coming!"[1]

The Disciples of Christ

The Whitneys and almost all the other converts in Ohio were members of a new society called the "Disciples of Christ." They were called the "Campbellites" because of their two outstanding leaders, Thomas and Alexander Campbell. There was no church in the world that taught so many doctrines of the restoration as the "Campbellites" had been teaching for a few years. Just as surely as Parley P. Pratt found a few people prepared in eastern Canada, awaiting the message he took them, so did the four missionaries who paused in Kirtland during their journey to the Indians in western Missouri.

The work of preparation that had been accomplished in eastern Canada was very meager in comparison with that which the "Campbellite" reformers had achieved in northern Ohio. When Heber C. Kimball set Parley P. Pratt apart for his mission to Canada he promised him that "there thou shalt find a people prepared for the fullness of the Gospel, and they shall receive thee." Yet that preparation was limited, indeed, and the number who received his message was a mere handful in comparison with the hundreds who readily accepted the message in Ohio.

A few years later Wilford Woodruff was inspired to go to Herefordshire in England, where a work of preparation was in progress. In a few months he baptized eighteen hundred members, including forty-five preachers. In every case where groups similar to the "Toronto Society" and the "United Brethren" were contacted, their numbers were small and the work of preparation they had accomplished was restricted and limited in comparison

---

[1] History of the Church. 1, 146.

with the "Campbellite" reformation that had swept the Western Reserve.

The first revelation given in behalf of Sidney Rigdon announced a truth that cannot be fully understood without a knowledge of the reformers in Ohio. It contained these words, "Behold thou wast sent forth, even as John, to prepare the way before me." There was no other place in the world where the Church leaders could have turned at that time and found a people prepared and doctrines being taught that were so comparable to the revealed teachings of the restoration.

There was a legend among the early Teutonic tribes in central Europe that a goddess in heaven known as the Nom-Mother, was assigned to keep watch over the earth and send the spirits from heaven to earth at the time they could do the most good. The poet Edwin Markham had this theory in mind, when he wrote his masterpiece, "Lincoln, the Great Commoner," which begins with these lines:

> When the Norn-Mother saw the Whirlwind Hour,
> Greatening and darkening as it hurried on,
> She bent the strenuous Heavens and came down,
> To make a man to meet the mortal need,

The work of preparation that had been accomplished on the Western Reserve was nothing short of miraculous. It was as great a mission in the spirit of Elias as had been accomplished before by the great reformers in Europe. It was a master stroke of diplomacy when Joseph Smith went home with Sidney Rigdon and Edward Partridge, where he and his missionaries were soon to baptize hundreds from the "Campbellite" fold and build a powerful branch in a short time, an accomplishment that could not have been achieved elsewhere in the world.

For a complete knowledge of Church history and the growth of the Doctrine and Covenants we must know the story of the "Disciples of Christ" on the Western Reserve. They were teaching so many things that the Mormons later taught that, they accused Joseph Smith of stealing most of his religious pattern from them. Moreover, most of these common doctrines were not a part of the restoration at the dawn of 1831 when the Prophet moved among them. Upon this subject a thesis was recently written in an eastern university for a Ph. D., degree, "The Influence of the Frontier on Joseph Smith."

In 1807 Thomas Campbell, a Scotch-Irish preacher arrived in America to carry out the reformation he had dreamed about in Ireland. Two years later his son Alexander arrived and gave his full support to his father's reformation. They were weary of the strife that existed in the sects of Christendom, hoping to promote unity by restoring the primitive church of the New Testament.[2]

The Campbells sought to be bound only by the scriptures and not by any human creeds. Since they practiced baptism by immersion they were invited to join the Baptist Association, which they did, in 1813.

Because of friction the Campbells withdrew from that association in 1830. The most popular theme of the reformers was the "Restoration of the Ancient Order of Things." Their ministers were soon preaching this message in the hamlets on the frontier, where they found many disciples. In 1830 many Baptists united with the reformation. Sidney Rigdon, his brother-in-law Adamson Bentley, and many other Baptist preachers followed Thomas Campbell into his expanding society.

In 1820 Rigdon accepted the new ideas of this reformation and was, licensed to preach the same year. "He was a man of extraordinary native eloquence," his Campbellite friends wrote of

---

[2] Daryl Chase, *Christianity Through the Centuries*. p. 242.

him, and soon made his name well known. Along with Bentley he gave himself to the new ideas until 1830 when he fell away to Mormonism. By these men, in cooperation with Walter Scott; the majority of the Baptist churches on the Western Reserve were permeated with the new teaching."[3]

The Campbells were brilliant, aggressive, and courageous. They taught many revolutionary doctrines that were not taught by any other denomination at that time. They insisted that there had been an apostasy and that the primitive church would be restored; that ministers would be endowed with the holy authority that the ancient apostles possessed. They taught that baptism by immersion was for the remission of sins, a new doctrine even to the Baptists.

Some of the Baptist factions had practiced the, laying on of hands, feet-washing, the anointing of the sick, weekly communion, and other revolutionary doctrines as a part of their plan to restore the ancient order of things. For a time they even anointed apostles, but the custom soon met with disapproval and was discontinued.

Then as now the motto of the "Campbellites" was "Where the Bible speaks we speak and where the Bible is silent we are silent," yet their ministers could not agree on where the Bible "spoke." In 1829 they started a new publication, its very name filled with the spirit of the time, *The Millennial Harbinger*, which soon became a powerful instrument in carrying the new philosophy to many people. The fly leaf, first printed on the eve of that historic year of restoration—1830—bore this striking prophecy of restoration:

> And I saw another angel fly in the midst of heaven, having the everlasting gospel to preach unto them that dwell on the

---

[3] Errett Gates and E. B. Hurlbert. *The Early Relation and Separation of Baptists and Disciples*, p. 86; A. S. Hayden, *History of the Disciples in the Western Reserve*, pp. 31, 61, 77.

earth, and to every nation, and kindred, and tongue, and people, Saying with a loud voice, Fear God and give glory to him; for the hour of his judgment is come.

This new movement has never been given its full credit as a forerunner, preparing the way for the restoration. In all the hamlets near Kirtland, Rigdon, Bentley, and Scott had long been preaching many of the doctrines of the restoration-the same doctrines that the four missionaries expounded when they paused in Kirtland to tell the old friends of Elder Pratt of the restoration of the ancient order of things. One of the most popular of the common beliefs were the first "five principles." The "Campbellite" reformers always stressed them—"First faith, repentance, baptism, remission of sins, and the gift of the Holy Ghost."

Scott often stopped children on the street, asked them to raise one hand and he would count the five principles on their fingers, urging them to hasten home and tell their parents about the five principles and invite them to attend their public meeting that night. While preaching he would often raise his left hand "Using his thumb for faith, and so on; then contrast it with the five points of Calvinism; and thus make it so plain that the little boys could carry it home."

These reformers had built up such strong branches on the Western Reserve that it is little wonder that the restoration was received with such willingness. This people was prepared for the truth. They had heard about the first five principles; all salaried "hirelings" in the church had been denounced; a name that reflected the primitive Christian Church 'was recommended; the Lord's Supper was observed weekly, the apostasy was taught, and the restoration of the ancient order of things was prayerfully anticipated.[4]

In every hamlet on the Western Reserve the missionaries

---

[4] Winffred B. Garrison, *Religion Follows the Frontier*, pp. 59-67.

from this new society were preaching the popular creeds to audiences on the street corners, in cottage meetings, and in large chapels. Hundreds of free thinkers on the frontier embraced the new religion and looked forward to a full restoration of the ancient order of things." Joseph Smith moved into the very strongholds of this denomination, and soon convinced hundreds that the "restoration" the Campbell disciples had been expecting was now in progress under a different name and far more glorious than they had anticipated.

Typical of the sermons and writings from the leaders of that reform movement, we quote the following from, their popular literature:

> The spirit of God has been moving the minds of such men as Glos, Sandeman, and others to plead for a restoration of the ancient Gospel.[5]

> Hence we cherish the hope and breathe the prayer that the spirit of missionary zeal and of primitive simplicity may shed its effulgence on our American Zion.[6]

> It is obvious to the most superficial observer, who, is at all acquainted with the state of Christianity and of the church of the New Testament, that much, very much is wanting, to bring the Christianity and the church of the present day up to that standard....[7]

> All wise and good men expect a millennium, or a period of great happiness upon earth. They all argue that greater light than that hitherto possessed will be universally enjoyed. They do not merely expect a universal subjugation of all nations, kindreds, and tongues, to the Lord Jesus; they do not merely expect a state of harmony, perfect peace and union among all the citizens of heaven; but they look for a

---

[5] W.T. Moore, *A Comprehensive History of the Disciples of Christ*, p. 432.
[6] *The Christian Baptist*, (Preface).
[7] Ibid., p 127.

vast accumulation of light and know, ledge, religious, moral, and political, They do not, however, expect a new Bible or any new revelation of the Spirit, but only a more clear and comprehensive knowledge of the sacred writings which we now enjoy. This belief and expectation of all wise and good men, is unequivocally declarative of the conviction that the scriptures are not now generally understood, and that there are new discoveries of the true and genuine meaning of the sacred records yet to be made.

I am fully aware of the difficulties under which these Christians withdrew from the popular establishments. They were sick of frivolous formalities, tired with the poor entertainment of insipid speculation and traditional prescriptions, and desirous of understanding and living upon the Book of God. But they had lost the key of interpretation, or rather they withdrew from the popular establishments with much esteem for the Bible, but with the textuary notions expounding it. They did not know or feel that when they commenced interpreting for themselves, they were only using the tools which they carried from the pulpits which they had forsaken. A restoration of the ancient order of things is all that is necessary to the happiness and usefulness of Christians.[8]

But a restoration of the ancient order of things, it appears is all that is contemplated by the wise disciples of the Lord.

Many there were who, wearied with the denominational strife, and restive under ecclesiastical domination, awaited a prophet whose aim was spiritual emancipation, and whose strong and fearless leadership they could trust.[9]

An era is just at the door, which will be known as the Regeneration for a thousand years to come. The Lord Jesus will soon rebuild Jerusalem, and raise up the tabernacle of David which has so long been in ruins. Let the church pre-

---

[8] Ibid., p. 128.
[9] T. W, Grafton, *Life of Alexander Campbell*, p. 116.

pare herself for the return of her Lord, and see that she make herself ready for his appearance. But the preparations of a people for the coming of the Lord must be the result of the restoration of the ancient gospel and order of things....[10]

Besides, do not the experience of all the religious-the observations of the intelligent-the practical result of all creeds, reformations, and improvements-and the expectation and longings of society—warrant the conclusion that either some new revelation, or some new development of the revelation, of God must be made, before the hopes and expectations of all true Christians can be realized, or Christianity save and reform the nations of the world? We want the old gospel back, and sustained by the ancient order of things; and this alone, by the blessings of the Divine Spirit, is all that we do want, or can expect, to reform and save the world.

For a divine warrant has always been essential to any acceptable worship. The question, "Who has required this at your hands?" must always be answered by a "Thus saith the Lord," before an offering of mortal man can be acknowledged by the Lawgiver of the universe. "In vain," said the Great Teacher. "Do you worship God, teaching for doctrines the commandments of men."

Still a regular and constant ministry was needed among the Jews, and is yet needed among the Christians; and both of these by divine authority.[11]

The "signs of the times" indicate some wonderful revolution in the state of the world. This every candid and careful observer must see. To close our eyes therefore, against it, is to act as the Ephesians did when the uproar was raised by the teachings of Paul. [12]

---

[10] Alexander Campbell, *The Christian System*, p. 310.
[11] Ibid., p. 20.
[12] *The Christian Baptist*, VI:517.

We have to pattern after the first (church) as well as we can, but we can never equal it. With all our efforts the great disparity will ever remain, and could the apostles and primitive Christians be here, they would doubtless weep at beholding it.[13]

We are convinced, fully convinced, that the whole head is sick, and the whole heart faint of modern fashionable Christianity. It is not the prescription of zealously engaging in all the projects of converting the world, recommended by the popular clergy, that will heal the diseases of the people; but it is an abandonment of every human scheme, and a submission to learn and study Christianity as developed in the Bible. This is the course, and the only course, that will effect a cure and renovate the constitution.[14]

And while I write and labor as I do, he that knows the hearts of all flesh knows that I do it from the fullest conviction from his oracles that the Christianity of our day is a corrupt Christianity, and that the ancient order of things is lost sight of in almost all denominations of professing Christians.[15]

It is a thing equally deplorable and dangerous, that there are as many creeds as there are opinions among men; as many doctrines as inclinations; and as many sources of blasphemy as there are faults among us; because we make creeds arbitrarily, and explain them as arbitrarily. And as there is but one faith, so is there but one God, one Lord, and one baptism. We renounce this one faith when we make so many different creeds; and that diversity is the reason why we have no true faith among us. We can not be ignorant that since the Council of Nice, we have done nothing but make creeds.[16]

The teachings of the "Disciples" had certainly opened the

---

[13] *Millennial Harbinger*, V:40.
[14] *The Christian Baptist*, 1:33.
[15] Ibid., IV: 285,
[16] Ibid., IV: 296.

way for the divine truths that were soon to be taught in every hamlet on the frontier. This work of preparation was well acknowledged and explained in the first revelation that was given in behalf of Sidney Rigdon when he arrived in Fayette to interview the Prophet and ascertain if this were the true restoration about which, he and his colleagues had been dreaming:

> I have looked upon thee and thy works. I have heard thy prayers, and prepared thee for a greater work.
>
> Thou art blessed, for thou shalt do great things. Behold thou wast sent forth, even as John, to prepare the way before Elijah which should come, and thou knewest it not.
>
> Thou didst baptize by water unto repentance, but they received not the Holy Ghost;
>
> But now I give unto thee a commandment, that thou shalt baptize by water, and they shall receive the Holy Ghost by the laying on of the hands, even as the apostles of old.
>
> And it shall come to pass that there shall be a great work in the land, even among the Gentiles, for their folly and their abominations shall be made manifest in the eyes of all people.[17]

We fail to catch the full significance of those words until we know the doctrines of the "Disciples" and realize how they were preparing the people for the truths of the restoration. In that same revelation Sidney was instructed to become a scribe for Joseph "and the scriptures shall be given, even as they are in mine own bosom, to the salvation of mine elect."

This was welcome news to the new disciple, since his former leaders had long been preaching that the Bible should be revised. In fact they had published a revision of the scriptures and had

---

[17] Doctrine and Covenants 35:3-7.

insisted that the Protestant Bible was poorly translated. Most ministers would have rebelled against Joseph Smith if they had been told, the day they first met him, that they were expected to assist in the revision of the Bible. Sidney had been teaching that doctrine for a decade and was anxious to hasten into the welcome labor at once.

"The Field Is White"

In any other region but northern Ohio the Church would have had a hard time getting a foothold. Their doctrines were so new and revolutionary to those of orthodox Christianity that a wave of persecution would have engulfed them, but there were thousands on the Western Reserve who were well prepared for the divine message.

During the summer of 1828, Bishops Scott, Rigdon, and Bentley baptized. 800 persons in the vicinity of Kirtland. In every instance "baptism was connected with the promise of the remission of sins and the gift of the Holy Ghost," a doctrine that was not being taught elsewhere.[18]

We must glean many facts from the official publications of the "Campbellites" to show what a comprehensive preparation they had made for the restoration. Their prolific writings abound with such teachings and historical sidelights as the following:

> If any man, therefore, contend that human creeds are necessary to the unity of the church, he at the same time and by all the same arguments, contends that the scriptures of the Holy spirit are insufficient—that is, imperfect or defective. Every human creed is based upon the inadequacy, that is, the imperfection of the holy scriptures.[19]

---

[18] Gates and Huribert, *op. cit.*, p. 34.
[19] *The Christian Baptist*, p. 134.

The historian Grafton assures us that the people on the restless frontier were well prepared for such a reform as the Campbells started. "Many there were," he was convinced, "who, wearied with the denominational strife, and restive under ecclesiastical domination, awaited a prophet whose aim was spiritual emancipation, and whose strong and fearless leadership they could trust."[20]

This is typical of the voluminous writings of the "Campbellites" on the various subjects of the restoration. For years their publications had been crowded with this philosophy. Their sermons shook the hearers out of their lethargy and complacency, firing them with a zeal to look forward to something greater than any of the churches offered them, and created a spirit of discontent in the churches on the frontier. By 1830 the restless people on the frontier were eagerly awaiting something new in religion. The "Campbellites" had said so much about the restoration of the ancient order and an inspired ministry going abroad, endowed with the authority that the ancient disciples possessed, with authority to correct the evils in the churches, revise the Bible, and restore the primitive religion, that the thousands on the Western Reserve expected just such a message as the Mormons brought them.

"Mark it well," declared one of their preachers, "we are the only people who would tolerate, or who ever did tolerate any person to continue as a reformer or a restorer amongst us.[21] "It was the baptism for the remission of sins that distinguished the baptisms of these reforming preachers from ordinary Baptist baptisms.[22] Sidney Rigdon, before his defection to the Mormons, began to advocate the restoration of the ancient communism as practiced in the church at Jerusalem. These extremes were not widespread. They were the inevitable phenomena connected with

---

[20] Thomas W. Grafton, *Life of Alexander Campbell*, p. 116,
[21] Gates and Hurlbert, *op. cit.*, p. 520.
[22] Ibid., p. 66.

an earnest effort to restore the primitive faith and practice.[23] This was a time of preparation. Just as surely as John the Baptist went forth preaching a doctrine of preparation for greater things to come, so did the zealous "Campbellites" preach a preparatory message to the colonists on the Ohio frontier. Concerning other reform movements at the same time it has been wisely said:

> Protestant churches were departing from the principles of the great Reformation in their faith and practice. These are indications that the spirit of reform was in the air. It belonged to the spirit of the age. None of them have come to such widespread influence or strength as the movement led by the Campbells.
>
> Besides these organized and affiliated bodies there were single churches that sought the New Testament basis, which were entirely out of fellowship with other churches; one in Baltimore under the leadership of a Mr. Duncan; one in Philadelphia under the leadership of Mr. Chambers; and one in Gettysburg, Pa., under the leadership of Mr. McLean. All three were Presbyterian churches. They renounced the authority of the Westminster Confession of Faith and the Presbystery in 1825, and established themselves upon New Testament ground. About 1818-1820 a church in New York was organized independently, with the Bible as the only rule of faith and practice, and sought to restore the exact order of the apostolic churches. This church heard of other similar organizations from time to time, and entered into correspondence with them to ascertain the faith and practice of each. The following churches were heard from-one in Edinburg, one in Manchester, and one in Dublin.[24]

"All agreed to the desirability of the union of all Christians, but did not agree as to the way of it, namely: By restoring apostolic

---

[23] Ibid., p. 75.
[24] Ibid., p. 84.

Christianity. It is the work of God, who hath raised up a prophet in these last days in the person of the Bethany sage."[25]

The following quotations reveal the spirit of the time and the great work of preparation that had been achieved on the Ohio frontier:

> During the year 1830, which was pre-eminently the year of separation of Baptists from Reformers, reports are numerous and dark of the state of affairs in Baptist churches. Surely it was a dark period when many times the half of a congregation or the majority of it, went over to the Reformers; when parts of associations, and the strongest parts, declared for "the ancient order of things." It meant, in many instances, not merely the weakening of Baptist churches but the closing of church doors, the cessation of public services, the breaking up of old associations, and the estrangement of friends. Not the least was the reproach such divisions brought upon the Christian religion before an unsympathetic world. Baptist papers were full of warnings, reproaches, and lamentation over the inroads of the new teachings. The following lamentation is taken from a report of the state of things in Tennessee by Mr. M. Connico:
>
> "My beloved brethren:—Campbellism has carried away many whom I thought firm. These wandering stars and clouds without water ever learning and never able to come to the knowledge of the truth, make proselytes much more the children of the devil than they were before. o Lord! hear the cries and see the tears of the Baptists; for Alexander hath done them much harm. The Lord reward him according to his works. Look at the Creaths of Kentucky. Look at Anderson, Craig, and Hopwood, of Tennessee. See them dividing churches and spreading discord, and constitution churches out of excommunicated members. Such shuffling-such lying—such slandering-such evil—speaking—such

---

[25] Ibid., p. 87.

dissembling—such downright hypocrisy and all under the false name of reformation."

If merciless hostility ever bears witness to the success of a thing, we need only consult the number, the eminence, and the bitterness of his opposers to conclude that he had achieved the highest degree of success before 1830, Yet both friend and foe alike testified to his success. In this instance, as in many others, a man's worst foes shall be they of his own house. The Baptists fought the progress of the new ideas more than any other people. They wrote replies, issued decrees, excommunicated his followers, defamed his character, locked church doors against him and his missionaries, ostracized and proscribed them in various quarters, and burned his books and theirs. Such treatment only fanned his ardor and made him friends.[26]

The reforming and restoring "Disciples" soon became a great missionary society. In every hamlet in the Western Reserve their missionaries were declaring the good news of restoration. For a decade their prolific writings had been scattered broadcast by their numerous publications which were well received by the daring and adventurous settlers on the fringe of society who were far removed from the stiff and rigid theological patterns that held the worshipers in their strong embrace in the eastern cities. Just as surely as the frontiersmen broke the wilderness they also broke the fetters of religious dogma and tradition that held them bound to the formal rituals of the established churches. Akin to the great reformation that had swept Europe in the days of Luther, Calvin, and Knox, a minor movement had spread over the American frontier. It is significant that their most far reaching results had been achieved in Ohio, and their strongholds were the very hamlets in which the Mormons would soon reap a bounteous harvest.

For a decade the woods had resounded with the sermons of

---

[26] Ibid., pp. 88, 100, 101.

the determined reformers. Their sermons, hundreds of them, resembled the sermons that were soon to be preached by the Elders of the Church after the restoration had burst upon the world in its full glory. The following quotation from a renowned "Campbellite" historian is typical of volumes of sermons and writings that were popular upon the frontier, all of which had a tremendous effect upon the freethinking wilderness breakers and prepared them for the divine truths that were soon to follow:

> The day of light, so illustrious in its beginning, became cloudy. The Papacy arose and darkened the heavens for a long period, obscuring the brightness of the risen glory of the Sun of righteousness so that men groped in darkness. By the reformation of the 17th century that dark cloud was broken in fragments; and though the heavens of gospel light are still obscured by many clouds-the sects of various names-the promise is that "at evening-time it shall be light." The primitive gospel in its effulgence and power, is yet to shine out in its original splendor to regenerate the world ...
>
> Here were Methodists, no longer Methodists, but still Christians; Baptists surrendering the title, yet holding the Head, even Christ; Restorationists, giving up their fruitless and faulty speculation, now obedient to the faith once delivered to the saints; Bible Christians, recovered from their negative gospel to the apostle's method of preaching, together with very many other forms of religions belief, all rejoicing together, perfectly united in the same mind and the same judgment.[27]

The Voice of a "Campbellite" Historian Is Heard

The story of the conversion of Sidney Rigdon has been well told in the records of the Church, but the following account from the pen

---

[27] Hayden, *op. cit.*, pp. 36, 162.

of a "Campbellite" historian is interesting and sheds a flood of light and local color on this subject.

Sidney Rigdon was an orator of no inconsiderable abilities. In person, he was full medium height, rotund in form; of countenance, while speaking, open and winning, with a little cast of melancholy. His action clear and musical. Yet he was an enthusiast, and unstable. His personal influence with an audience was very great; but many, with talents far inferior, surpassed him in judgment and permanent power with the people. He was just the man for an awakening.

The trumpet which blew gave no uncertain sound. It was the old jubilee trumpet, first sounded by the fishermen of Galilee on the day of Pentecost, announcing glad tidings to the nations that the year of release from bondage in sin had now come, calling ransomed sinners to return, freely pardoned, to their homes. They spoke with authority, for the word they delivered was not theirs, but that of Jesus Christ. The whole community was quickly and thoroughly aroused. Many turned to the Lord. The first person to accept the offered boon and lead the people to. Christ, was an intelligent young man, M. S. Clapp, then in his twenty-first year, son of judge Clapp. His older brother, Thomas J. Clapp, had been baptized in June previous. Twenty persons were baptized the first time they repaired to the Jordan. The immediate result of the meeting was the conversion of over fifty souls to the Lord Jesus.

It is impossible to describe the agitation of the public mind. The things which they heard were so new, yet so clearly scriptural, that, while some hesitated and many wondered, they could not gainsay it; and nearly the whole church accepted cordially the doctrine of the Lord, exchanged their "articles" for the new covenant as the only divine the basis for Christ's church, and abandoned unscriptural titles and church names, choosing to be known simply as the disciples of Christ.

From Mentor they went to Kirtland, where almost an equal in gathering awaited them. The fields were white for the harvest. At the first baptizing here, twenty souls were lifted into the kingdom. Others followed, and soon the numbers so increased that a separate organization became a necessity—so mightily prevailed the word of the Lord.

The news of this great overturn spread quickly through the country, up and down the lake shore. Bentley went to Painsville. The rumor of the revival in Mentor preceded him, with some exaggerated and perverted accounts of the preaching. He delivered a few discourses on the first principles of the gospel, and left them to leaven the minds of his hearers. The church now contained' over a hundred members.

Few communities have been so stable; the families here named have composed the staple of membership, and the support of the church from that time to the present. This congregation has long stood as a lighthouse. It was shaken as by a tempest under the outbreak of Mormonism; but it is to be noted that few of its members were led astray. While the church in Kirtland, with less experience, and more immediately in Rigdon's power, became enguphed, and has never since been recovered, the church in Mentor, with stronger material, withstood the shock. They were much aided in their resistance by the presence of Elder Thomas Campbell, who spent several months there and in. the vicinity during the agitation which it produced.

Bro. A. P. Jones and J. J. Moss, equally bold and with more learning, was his true yoke-fellow. They were both teaching in the vicinity, of Kirtland, when Mormonism invaded the place, and hand in hand, though young, they often put its champions to flight.

This was in the fall of 1830. This coarse imposture was not born of chance. Characterized by much that is gross, and accompanied by practices repulsive for their lowness and vulgarity, it yet had a plan and an aim, and it was led on by a master spirit of delusion. It marked out its own coarse, and premeditated its points of attack. Its advent in Mentor was not accidental. Its four emissaries to the "Lamanites" in the West, like the four evil messengers from the Euphrates (Rev. ix: 15), had Rigdon in their eye before leaving Palmyra, N.Y. On. his part, Rigdon, with pompous pretense, was travailing with expectancy of some great event soon to be revealed to the surprise and astonishment of mankind. Gifted with very fine powers of mind, an imagination at once fertile, glowing and wild to extravagance, with temperament tinged with sadness and bordering on credulity, he was prepared and preparing others for the voice of some mysterious event soon to come.

The discomfiture he experienced at the hands of Mr. Campbell at Austintown, when seeking to introduce his common property scheme, turned him away mortified, chagrined and alienated, This was only two and a half months before he received, in peace, the messengers of delusion. Another fact: A little after this, the same fall, and before the first emissaries of the Mormon prophet came to Mentor, Parley P. Pratt, a young preacher of some promise from Lorain County, a disciple under Rigdon's influence, passing through Palmyra, the prophet's home, turned aside to see this great sight. He became an easy convert. Immediately an embassy is prepared, composed of this same, P. P. Pratt, Oliver Cowdery and two others, for the "Lamanites."

The next scene opens in Mentor. About the middle of November, came two footmen with carpet bags filled with copies of the Book of Mormon, stopped at Rigdon's. What passed that night between him and these young prophets no pen will reveal; but interpreting events came rapidly on. Next morning, while judge Clapp's family were at breakfast, in came Rigdon, and in an excited manner said: "Two men came to my house last night on a c-u-r-i-o-u-s-. mission;" prolonging the word in a strange manner, When thus awakened, all around the table looking up, he proceeded to narrate how some men in Palmyra, N. Y., had found, by the direction of an angel, certain plates inscribed with mysterious characters; that by the same heavenly visitant, a young man, ignorant of letters, had been led into the secret of deciphering the writing on the plates; that it made known the origin of the Indian tribes; with other matters of great interest to the world and that the discovery would be of such importance as to open the way for the introduction of the Millennium. Amazement! They had been accustomed to his stories about the Indians, much more marvelous than credible, but that strange statement, made with an air both of wonder and credulity, overcame their patience. "It's all a lie," cried out Matthew, quite disconcerting the half apostate Rigdon; and this future Aaron of the new prophet retired.

These two men who came to Rigdon's residence, were the young preacher before named, P. P. Pratt, intimately acquainted with Rigdon, and therefore, doubtless chosen to lead the mission, and Oliver Cowdery. This Mr. Cowdery was one of the three original witnesses to Mormonism; Martin Harris and David Whitmer were the other two. Harris was the first scribe to. record the new Bible at the dictation of Smith; but through carelessness he suffered the devil to steal 116 pages of the manuscript, and then Cowdery was chosen in his stead.

These men stayed with Rigdon all the week. In the neighborhood lived a Mr. Morely, a member of the church in Kirtland, who, acting on the community principles, had established a "family." The new doctrines of having "all things in common," and of restoring miracles to the world as a fruit and proof of true faith, found a ready welcome by this incipient "community." They were all, seventeen in number, re-immersed in one night into this new dispensation.

At this, Rigdon seemed much displeased. He told them what they had done was without precedent or authority from the Scriptures, as he showed, baptized penitenial believers for the remission of sins. When pressed, they said what they had done was merely at the solicitation of those persons. Rigdon called on them for proofs of the truth of their book and mission. They related the manner in which they obtained faith, which was by praying for a sign, and an angel appeared to them. Rigdon here showed them from Scripture the possibility of their being deceived: "For Satan himself is transformed into an angel of light." "But." said Cowdery, "do you think if I should go to my Heavenly Father, with all sincerity, and pray to him, in the name of Jesus Christ, that he would not show me an angel-that he would suffer Satan to deceive me." Rigdon replied: "If the Heavenly Father has ever promised to show you an angel to confirm anything, he would not suffer you to be deceived; for John says: "If we ask any thing according to his will, he heareth us." "But," he continued, "if you should ask the Heavenly Father to show you an angel, when he has never promised such a thing if the devil never had an opportunity before of deceiving you, you give him one now."

This was a word in season, fitly spoken; yet, strange enough!

Two days afterward he was persuaded to tempt God by asking this sign. The sign appeared, and he was convinced that Mormonism was of God! According to his own reasoning, therefore,. Satan appeared to him as an angel of light. But he now imputed his former reasoning to pride, incredulity, and the influence of the Evil One."

The next Sunday Rigdon, accompanied by Pratt and Cowdery, went to Kirtland to his appointment. He attempted to preach; but with the awful blasphemy in his heart, and the guilt of so shameless an apostasy on his conscience, how could he open his mouth in the name of the insulted Jesus. The eloquent lips which never stammered before, soon became speechless, and his tongue was dumb. The faithless watchman, covered with the shame of his fall, surrendered his pulpit and congregation to the prey of wolves. Cowdery and Pratt did most of the preaching; and that day, both Mr. and Mrs. Rigdon, with many of the members of the church in Kirtland, were baptized into the new faith.

Though coming into Ohio first among the disciples, and introduced to their attention in a well-planned and artful manner, very few of the leading members were for a moment deceived. After its first approach, it boasted of few converts from any of our churches. Rigdon, Pratt and Orson Hyde, the last two young and but little known, were the only preachers who gave it countenance.

The opposition to it was quick on its feet, in rank, and doing effective work to check the imposture. J. J. Moss, at the time a young school-teacher in the place, pelted them, but not with grass. Isaac Moore stood up, and became a shield to many. The vigilance of the Clapps prevented any serious inroads into the church of Mentor. Collins forbade its approach to Chardon, and it merely skulked around it hills. Alexander P. Jones was there also, young, shrewd, and skilled. In many an encounter he was left without a foe. But the misfortune governing the case was that many people, victims of excitement and credulity, and taught in nearly all pulpits to pray for faith, now found themselves met on their own grounds, and so finding an emotion or impulse answerable to an expected response from heaven, dared not dispute the answer to their own prayers, and were hurried into the vortex. The reason the delusion made little progress among the Disciples, save only at Kirtland, where the way it was paved by the common-stock principle, is to be found in the cardinal principle everywhere taught and accepted among them, that faith is founded on testimony.

The venerable Thomas Campbell, hearing of the defection of Rigdon and the progress this silly delusion was making, came quickly to the front. He spent much of the winter in Mentor and vicinity. His wise counsels and great weight of influence interposed an effectual barrier against its encroachments. He addressed a communication to Rigdon so firm, so fatherly and characteristic, that the reader shall have the pleasure of perusing it. Its great length will apologize for the omission of a portion of it. Soon after his return to Kirtland, Rigdon fulminated a pompous challenge to the world to disprove the new Bible. On this Mr. Campbell wrote him, as follows:

Mentor, February 4, 1831

Mr. Sidney Rigdon,

"Dear Sir:—It may seem strange, that instead of a confidential and friendly visit, after so long an absence, I should thus address, by letter, one whom for many years I have considered not only as a courteous and benevolent friend, but is a beloved brother and fellow-laborer in the gospel; but, alas! how changed, how fallen! Nevertheless, I should now have visited you, as formerly, could I conceive that my so doing would answer the important purpose, both to ourselves and to the public, to which we both stand pledged, from the conspicuous and important stations we occupy—you as the professed disciple and public teacher of the infernal Book of Mormon, and I as a professed disciple and public teacher of the supernal book of the Old and New Testaments of our Lord and Savior Jesus Christ, which you now say is superceded by the Book of Mormon—is become a dead letter; so dead that the belief and obedience of it, without the reception of the latter, is no longer available for salvation. To the disproof of this assertion, I understand you to defy the world. I here use the epithets infernal and supernal in, their primary and literal meaning, the former signifying from beneath, the latter from above, both of which are truly applied, if the respective authors may be accredited; of the later of which, however, I have no doubt. But, my dear sir, supposing you are sincere in your present, as in your former profession, neither yourself, your friends, nor the world are bound to consider you as more infallable in your latter than in your former confidence, any further than you can render good and intelligible reasons for your present certainty. This, I understand from your declaration on last Lord's day, you are abundantly prepared and ready to do. I, therefore, as in duty bound, accept the challenge, and shall hold myself in readiness, if the Lord permit, to meet you publicly, in any place, either in Mentor or Kirtland, or in any of the adjoining towns that may appear most eligible for the accommodation of the public. The sooner the investigation takes place the better for all concerned.

"The proposition that I have assumed, and which I mean to assume and defend against Mormonism and every other ism that has been assumed since the Christian era, is the all-sufficiency and the alone-sufficiency of the Holy Scriptures of the Old and New Testaments, vulgarly called the Bible, to make every intelligent believer wise to salvation, thoroughly furnished for any good work, This proposition, clearly and fully established, as I believe t most certainly can be, we have no more need for Quakerisim, Shakerism, Wilkinsonianism, Buchanism, Mormonism, or any other ism, than we have for three eyes, three ears, three hands, or three feet, in order to see, hear, work, or walk.[28]

The work of preparation had been accomplished on the Ohio frontier; the preparatory message had swept the Western Reserve, preparing thousands for the divine message that was soon to come, but the ones who had spread the new philosophy were the ones in whose camps the opposition would arise and from which the worst persecution would spread.

---

[28] Hayden., *op, cit.*, pp. 174, 197, 209-218.

Chapter VIII

JOSEPH SMITH REVISES THE BIBLE

Two months after the Book of Mormon came from the press the translator was instructed to commence an inspired revision of the scriptures. In June, 1830, the first part of the "Book of Moses" was revealed at the time he started to revise the book of Genesis. This valuable material was to be used as a preface to Genesis. At the close of the year when he was again free to devote a little time to the task of revision the latter part of the "Book of Moses" was revised. It was called the "Prophecy of Enoch."

When he was ready to undertake the inspired revision of the scriptures he purchased from B. B. Grand in a large, pulpit edition of the Bible which had been printed in 1828. It contained the Apocrypha, those seven books which were considered by the Protestants as questionable. They were inserted at the end of the Old Testament. This was the King James Version, the Bible of the Protestant world. After the documents that are now preserved in the Pearl of Great Price were revealed, he made a check mark with a pencil at the beginning and end of every verse he was changing. Then he would dictate and his scribe would write the corrections or additions. He wrote no footnotes or marginal notes in the Bible, all the changes being written by the secretary on a thick sheaf of paper he had prepared for the purpose.

During Sidney's visit at Fayette he was instructed "to write for him; and the scriptures shall be given, even as they are in mine own bosom, to the salvation of mine elect."[1] In the spirit of Elias he had been well prepared for such an assignment. It was not necessary for his religious pattern to be altered seriously before he could enter upon that labor. He had long been convinced of the need of such an inspired revision. When this revision was undertaken in the very strongholds of the "Campbellites" and a flood of new information was revealed it turned the reformers against the leaders of the restoration more than anything they had done up to that time. We must deviate long enough to explain the "Campbellite" philosophy in this regard and show why they resented having their "thunder" stolen, as they considered it.

Most Christians considered the Bible so perfect and correct that a revision of any kind was regarded as blasphemy. Joseph Smith could not have gone into many denominations, converted an educated orthodox minister and put him to work immediately as an assistant in the revision of the Bible. We have under estimated the great mission of preparation that was accomplished by the "Campbellites" in Ohio on the eve of the arrival of the Mormons in that region.

At that time the *Journal and Luminary*, a popular newspaper published in Cincinnati, Ohio said of this subject:

> So long as a disposition to alter the Bible was confined to erratic sects, such as Campbellites, Universalists, etc., we had no fears. Nothing better could be expected from such a source; but when a great evangelical denomination betrays a disposition to tamper with the English Bible, it is time to be alarmed for the purity of the Word of God.

This was typical of the general attitude throughout Christendom on that subject. People who regarded the Bible as a perfect, com-

---

[1] Doctrine and Covenants 35:20.

plete, and properly translated book of scripture would resent many of the teachings of the restoration. The Book of Mormon, the Doctrine and Covenants, as well as the sermons and writings of the Church leaders would be rejected because of their inference that the Christian scriptures were poorly translated and improperly preserved. The "Campbellites" were in full agreement with the critical quotations in the Book of Mormon, which would be regarded in most Christian denominations as un-Christian and blasphemous:

> ...For behold, they have taken away from the gospel of the Lamb many parts which are plain and most precious; and also many covenants of the Lord have they taken away.
>
> "And all this have they done that they might pervert the right ways of the Lord, that they might blind the eyes and harden the hearts of the children of men.
>
> Wherefore, thou seest that after the book hath gone forth through the hands of the great and abominable church, that there are many plain and precious things taken away from the book, which is the book of the Lamb of God.[2]

The Campbells Revise the Bible

In 1826 Alexander Campbell published a revision of the New Testament which he called *Living Oracles*. This was practically a reprint of a translation recently completed by three Scotch Presbyterian ministers. He took the liberty of publishing it under his name as "proprietor," and took other liberties in revising it to suit his fancy. This revision became very popular with his disciples and others who did not consider it blasphemy to revise the scriptures. In subsequent editions he made many additional changes,

---

[2] 1 Nephi 13:23-32.

not because the "original Greek" texts had changed, but because he had changed his religious belief. After he was baptized in "much water" by the Reverend Luce of the Baptist Church, he changed his New Testament to conform wholly to his new-found faith. In the future editions his translation spoke of "John the Immerser, immersing in the Jordan."

In other instances he was not reluctant to depart from the orthodox text and introduce radical changes, as the following examples testify:

> And she brought forth a masculine son. (Revelations 12:5)

> In those days appeared John the Immerser, who proclaimed in the wilderness of Judea, saying Reform, for the Reign of Heaven approaches. (Matthew 3:1-2)

> But I say unto you, whosoever is angry with his brother unjustly, shall be obnoxious to the judges; whosoever shall call him fool, shall be obnoxious to the council; but whosoever shall call him miscreant, shall be obnoxious to hell fire. (Matthew 5:22)

> And why do you observe the mote in your brother's eye, but are insensible of the splinter in your own eye? Or how dare you say to your brother, Let me take the mote out or your eye; when lo! you have a splinter in your own? Hypocrite, first take the splinter out of your own eye; then you will see clearly to take the mote out of your brother's eye. (Matthew 7:3)

> But whosoever hears these my precepts, and does them not, shall be compared to, a simpleton, who built his house upon the sand. (Matthew 7:25)

> Who though he was in the form of God did not affect to appear in divine majesty. (Phillipians 2:6-7)

> I tell you likewise, you are named Stone, and on this rock I will build my congregation, on which the gates of Hades shall not prevail. (Matthew 16:18)

In the fourth edition of his New Testament he added an appendix which contained this paragraph:

> From persons of sound biblical learning and candor, we have nothing to fear; but from all bigots and liberal critics we expect the same coarse treatment which has fallen to the lot of every translator from Jerome's time until the present day, March 1, 1833.

The Campbell reformers were daring, courageous, revolutionary. They were not bound by any religious pattern or theological precedents. "If we have the right to preach we have the right, to baptize," Alexander Campbell once remarked when asked about the authority he possessed. He and his father wrote and lectured extensively about biblical revision and fallibility. In the popular *Millennial Harbinger* he reprinted the following article, reminding his readers that it is a Christian duty to "guard the purity of that source." It gave him great satisfaction to reprint such materials as this:

> *Falsification of the Scriptures:*—A reverend gentleman in England, named Curtis, has recently made some appalling disclosures in relation to the careless and iniquitous manner in which the University editions of the Holy Bible, published by the King's printer, are put forth to the world. Mr. Curtis has exposed some enormous errors, and variations from the original text, as given in King James' time. Six hundred mistakes have been found in one book, and eight hundred in another! many of them, most important, and all of them inexcusable. Some of the grosser ones, which would seem to have been concerted and intentional, have been rife for forty

years. The true sense of Holy Writ, it is contended, has been greatly warped by these errors; and measures are in train to have them ratified, in all future editions of the scriptures published in England. It is stated that the churches in America have long since adopted the edition in question as a standard;-if so, it is of the last importance, we should conceive to import one of the corrected copies, now preparing, at the earliest period. The writer remarks, with much sorrowful feeling, that such perversions of the Sacred Word have given rise to more scoffers and infidels, than could have been otherwise produced by any other cause.

His comments on this article are interesting. As if with the voice of authority he offered this explanation:

In regard to the falsifications and mistakes of the Bible, noticed in the first article, there is great reason to fear that they extend beyond the "University Editions published by the King's Printer." In the multiplicity of editions we see every day palmed upon the world, without any sanction or authority whatever, by booksellers and societies and denominations and sects of all sorts, where is the security that the text may not be altered to suit the peculiar tenets of each particular sect, or marred by the carelessness or ignorance of the publishers? We have heard it asserted, and from the hurried manner in which these Bibles are multiplied almost to infinity, we believe it to be true, that many of the common editions are scandalously inaccurate, if not wilfully falsified, to sanction the peculiar tenets of the sects by whom they are published. The common people who have in a great degree lost their reverence and value for the Sacred Book, from the usual effects of too great plenty, receive it without enquiry, though there is no security whatever for its accuracy, and no sanction of church or state to guard against interpolation, corruption or mistake.

These things ought not to be. The Bible is too important a volume to be left thus at the mercy of ignorance, carelessness, or wilful interested falsification. It should come forth with the sanction of some high and responsible authority, and carry with it evidence that it has undergone the strict scrutiny of persons, whose learning and integrity sufficiently guaranty the public against deception and falsehood. As it is now, we really see no obstacle to publishing Bibles to suit any system of morals or religion; and whose precepts may outrage every principle of the Decalogue. Living as we do under a Government which neither interferes nor allows interference in religious matters, it is without doubt difficult, if not impossible, to prevent impositions of this kind, since there is no law that we know of to prevent a man from publishing any book he pleases under the denomination of the Holy Bible. Still the evil we speak of is not the less to be deplored; and we cannot but recommend it most earnestly to the attention of all those who would preserve the scriptures from degenerating by degrees into a heterogeneous jumble of contradictory and irreconcilable inconsistencies. The few doctrinal differences originating in the two translations of the Bibles of the Catholic and Protestant faiths, detract but little from the divinity of the Scriptures; but the eternal multiplication of these differences, must, in the end, entirely destroy their force and authority, and undermine the very foundation of our faith. When it is seen that they sanction the most opposite and incongruous opinions, and that those who agree in nothing under heaven, can find in the Scriptures authority for all their differences, it cannot but happen that reflecting minds will begin to doubt the infallibility of an oracle so liable to be misinterpreted.

While the golden plates were being translated, the Campbells were pleading for a revision of the scriptures. Their arguments were continued even after the revision of the Bible was completed by Joseph Smith. Such a doctrine was certainly not new on the Western Reserve. The following quotations show what a vast work of preparation had been done by the Campbells and their ministers in northern Ohio on the eve of the restoration:

> There is no commentator, theologian, critic, or man of letters, who has paid much attention to the common English version, who does not say that it needs correction and emendation. But how this is to be accomplished....
>
> And why does he call the common version "King James' Bible," when there are many thousand alterations in it? So rare is a pure copy of King James', that I presume Dr. Clelland never saw one. I have not leisure to count, but I will affirm on the comparisons which I have made, taking the ration of a single book, that there are more than ten thousand alterations in the Bible Society editions of the King's version, compared with a genuine King James' Bible!
>
> ...To look to England for any change in the present version of the English Bible, is out of the question. The relative situation of the Established and Dissenting Churches, is sufficient to satisfy any one, that while it subsists, there can be no agreement, even on such points as a reformation or the present English Bible, in matters not sectarian. We must, therefore, judge and act for ourselves; and as unquestionably the changes, that might be adopted in this country, would be sanctioned, for the most part, if not altogether, by the best English and Scotch commentators, we may indulge the hope that we might thus be instrumental in preparing the way in Great Britain, for an amendment of King James' Bible among themselves.

Alexander Campbell quoted the following text from a recent

translation of the scriptures by Dickenson, objecting seriously to that kind of translation:

> Moreover, there was a Pharisee, whose name was Nicodemus, a senator of the Jews. He came to Jesus by night, and said unto Him, Teacher, we know that thou art an instructor emanated from God; for no one can achieve these miracles which thou performest unless God be with him. Jesus answered and said to him, Indeed, I assure you, that except a man be reproduced, he cannot realize the reign of God. Nicodemus says to him, How can, a man be produced when he is mature? Can he again pass into a state of embryo, and be produced? Jesus replied. I most assuredly declare to you, that unless a man be produced of water and of the Spirit, he cannot enter the kingdom of God. That which is produced from the body is natural life, and that which is produced from the Spirit is spiritual life.[3]

The Campbell comments on the Dickenson revision of the Bible give one an idea of what he would think when Joseph Smith started to revise the scriptures, adding lengthy material and supplying such additional information as is found in the seventy-sixth section of the Doctrine and Covenants. In opposition to the Dickenson version he made these comments:

> As to the delicacy, (which appears the chief object of the translator,) I would ask whether this squeamishness and fastidiousness do not betray more indelicacy of thought than is found in the simple and unaffected language of nature. The prude is more scrupulous and affected than a woman of unsuspected virtue. The over nicety of the former excites suspicion, while the simplicity and artlessness of the latter exhibit a mind unpractised in the arts of deception. If it be indelicate to speak of being born again, it is equally so to speak of being born; and this translator, to be consistent with

---

[3] *Millennial Harbinger*, IV, 461.

himself, ought to exclude this word and all its relatives from the Bible. Instead of "Them who are born of woman," he ought to say, "Of them that are produced by women;" and instead of "Thou shalt not commit adultery," "Thou shalt not have criminal conversation with a married lady." But even this is too coarse for a gentleman of such refined taste. It would be better to leave out the commandment altogether than to offend the rules of politeness![4]

As the revision of the scripture progressed under the inspiration of heaven, the Mormon leaders eagerly read the new translations that appeared and perused the numerous comments that appeared in the press on that subject. In the official publication of the Church just one month before the inspired revision was completed, an article was printed which contained this appropriate paragraph, "O what a blessing, that the Lord will bestow the gift of the Holy Spirit upon the meek and humble, whereby they can know of a surety his words from the words of men! O that men would learn wisdom, and know that a house divided against itself cannot stand."[5]

The Campbells and their popular teachers had blazed the trail on the Western Reserve and convinced thousands that the King James Version had not been translated correctly or divinely protected and preserved. For a decade they had been preaching about the Bible almost exactly what Nephi had told the people in his day.[6]

In each revision of Campbell's *Living Oracles* he made many changes in the text, not because the original Greek had changed, but because he was being influenced by the Unitarian creeds. He was criticized by his enemies because of the continuous revisions he was making, yet it convinced the thousands who regarded him as a great reformer that the Bible was not a static, sealed book, but

---

[4] Ibid., IV. 402, 522.
[5] *The Evening and Morning Star*, June, 1833.
[6] 1 Nephi 13:20-32.

should be subject to periodic and continuous revision and improvement.

In defense of his extensive revision of the translation by the three scholars in Ireland, and in praise of William Tyndale's translation which was so freely copied by the translators of 1611, he wrote:

> I think it will do much to expand the too contracted minds of many of the leaders of the people on the subject of New and Old Versions. It will correct much of that blind and implicit homage paid to the King's translators and translation, and cannot fail to convince the most prejudiced eulogists of the piety and eminent proficiency in ancient and sacred literature of the authors of the common version, that they have been rendering honor where it was not due, and ignorantly withholding it from the real author of the common version, to whom it was justly due: for certainly there is no man of good sense and of ordinary candor, who, after examining and comparing William Tyndal's Testament with the common, that will not acknowledge that William Tyndal is the real author of the King's version; or, in other words, that the King's translators were no translators at all, but simply copyists of Tyndal and collator of other Protestant versions. My edition of Campbell, MacKnight, and Doddridge's version, is fully as much my version as the common version is that of King James' "forty seven eminent Divines."[7]

It is amazing what a preparatory work was done by the "Campbellites" on the Ohio frontier. In the spirit of Elias they had prepared thousands of independent, freethinking Christians for the message the Mormons were soon to bring them. There was no place in America where such work of preparation had been so successfully pushed forward. It was wisely and truthfully said to Sidney Rigdon when he first met Joseph Smith, "Behold, thou

---

[7] *The Millennial Harbinger*, 1838, p. 92,

wast sent forth, even as John, to prepare the way before me, and before Elijah which should come, and thou knowest it not."[8]

In most Christian communities at that time they regarded the Bible as being so perfect that there was no room in their theological pattern for new scriptures such as the Book of Mormon, the Doctrine and Covenants, and the Pearl of Great Price. The "Campbellites" have not been given the full credit they deserve for the preparation they made for the truths of the restoration.

The Popular Solution

The following quotations indicate how the Bible was regarded in most Christian communities, and illustrates what a difficult task Mormon missionaries would have in adjusting their philosophy to that of the people who regarded the Bible as perfect, complete, and infallible:

> A Protestant Synod in Geneva, in 1675, asserted that the writer of Scripture is but a pen in the hand of God, and amanuensis of the Holy Spirit. The Scriptures throughout are verbally inspired, so that every one is just as God would have written it with His own hand. "Whatever is related by the Holy Spirit is absolutely true, whether it pertain to doctrine, morals, history, chronology, topography, or nomenclature."

Locke argued that the Bible "has God for its Author, salvation for its end, and truth, without any mixture of error, for its matter."

Gaussen says of this subject:

> God has dictated its pages during 16 centuries, to priests, kings, warriors, shepherds, tax-gatherers, fishermen, scribes and tent makers. Its first line, its last line, all its instructions,

---

[8] Doctrine and Covenants 35:3-7.

understood or not understood, are from the same author. Whoever the writers may have been . . . they have all written with a faithful, superintended hand, on the same scroll, under, the dictation of the same master, to whom a thousand years are as a day; such is the origin of the Bible.

Our sacred books contain no errors; all their writings are inspired of God . . . none of these words ought to be neglected, and we are called to respect them and to study them even to their least iota and to their least title, for these words of the Lord are pure words; as silver tried in a furnace of earth, they are perfect.[9]

Dr. Baylee, principal of St. Aidan's College, declared that in scripture "every scientific statement is infallibly accurate; all its histories and narratives of every kind are without inaccuracy. Its words and phrases have grammatical and philological accuracy, such as is possessed in no human composition." He further stated that, "Every syllable of it is just what it would be had God spoken from heaven without the intervention of any human agent."[10]

In 1861 Dean Burgon wrote about this subject:

The Bible is the very utterance of the Eternal; as much God's own word as if high heaven were open and we heard God speaking to us with human voice. Every book is inspired alike, and is inspired entirely. Inspiration is not a difference of degree, but of kind. The Bible is filled to overflowing with the Holy Spirit of God; the books of it, and the words of it and the very letters of it. The Bible is none other than the voice of Him that sitteth on the throne. Each book of it, every letter of it is the direct utterance of the Most High, supreme, absolute, faultless, unerring.

In a community where such a philosophy abounded there was

---

[9] S. L. R. Gausseu, *The Inspiration of the Bible*, p. 45.
[10] *Presbyterian Review*, II, 245.

no place for missionaries of the restoration. People who regarded the Bible in the manner expressed above would have regarded the Book of Mormon as un-Christian and blasphemous. In accepting the philosophy of the "Campbellites" one need not fling aside the Bible, but should see the shadow of mans hand that has fallen across many of its pages.

On the eve of the restoration the "Campbellites" were discussing a variety of subjects that were soon to be featured by the restored Church. In 1828 *The Christian Baptist* published this interesting comment:

> What mean these words, 1 Cor. XV. 29, "Else what shall they do who are baptized for the dead? If the dead rise not at all, why are they then baptized for the dead?"
>
> *Answer.* The next verse gives the key of interpretation. "And why stand we in jeopardy every hour?" Why should I, Paul, hazard my life in attesting the resurrection of Jesus Christ, if I had not the most unequivocal proof of his resurrection? Through this medium contemplate the preceding words. Only recollect that the word immerse is used frequently for sufferings. Jesus said, "I have an immersion to undergo, and how am I straightened till it be accomplished." I have to be immersed in an immense flood of sufferings. Also the phrase, "fallen asleep for Christ," is equivalent to dying for declaring faith in him. Now these criticisms regarded, and the elliptical verse 29, is plain and forcible—"If there be no resurrection from the dead, what shall they do who are immersed in afflictions and distress for believing and declaring that the dead will be raised? If the dead rise not at all, if they are not assured of their resurrection, why do they submit to be immersed in sorrows in the hope of a resurrection?"

A few years later another magazine published these comments on a subject that was soon to become a popular one, yet the true explanation was to be found only in the restored Church:

> Our early translators seem to have adopted the Roman Catholic notion of the gospel being preached to departed souls—"For whi for this thing it is preeched also to deed men."—Wickliff. "For unto this purpose verily was the gospel preeched also unto the deed."—Cranmer. Later translators have entertained very various opinions. Whitby, MacKnight, and Wakefield, consider "the dead" to be the Gentile world, "dead in sins." Wesley understands the apostle to say, "the gospel was preached ever since it was given to Adam, to them that are now dead, in their several generations." Scott thinks "the gospel had before this been preached to those (righteous persons) who were dead when the apostle wrote, either as martyrs for the truth, or dying in the course of providence." Knatchbull, by giving the words a scarcely justifiable construction, makes easy sense: "For this cause was the gospel preached to them that were dead, that they who lived according to men in the flesh may be condemned; but they who live according to God in the spirit may live." Boothroyd regards the dead as being martyrs, who, though they were condemned as to men in the flesh, yet lived as to God in the spirit. Adam Clarks takes the dead to be antedeluvians, who, although dead in sins and condemned to death by the righteous judgment of God, yet were respited and preached to, that they might "live a blessed life in eternity."[11]

One year before the "Words of Moses" were revealed at the time the inspired revision of the scriptures was undertaken, *The Christian Baptist* said of the subject of biblical revision:

> That God should send a message to mankind, on such an important subject as their eternal happiness, in language not intelligible to the most illiterate of them, is utterly incredible,

---

[11] *The London Christian Messenger*, 1851.

and to impute such conduct to the Diety is manifest impiety. If, then, the scriptures do contain a divine communication, it follows of course, that the words chosen by the Revealing Spirit must be the fittest to convey the ideas which he meant to communicate, that could be selected, and such as he knew to be perfectly intelligible to those to whom he addressed them, so far as be intended them to be understood. This granted, we are certainly authorized to consider the words of Scripture as they stand in the connexion formed by the Spirit, as calculated to convey, with perfect clearness and certainty, all the information which he designed to convey by them, and of course as insusceptible of additional clearness of certainty by and change of terms which man can devise.

And that King James' version needs a revision is just as plain to the learned and biblical student, as that the Scotch and English used in the sixteenth century, is not the language now spoken in these United States. And this may be made as plain to the common mind, as it is that the coat which suited the boy of twelve, will not suit the same person when forty years old. As the boy grows from his coat, so do we from the language of our ancestors.

A Choice Rendezvous

The selection of northern Ohio as a gathering place for the disciples of the restoration was a master stroke of diplomacy. Furthermore, the choice of that favorable region was a matter of divine inspiration. There was no other place in all the world where they could soon make so many converts and get a foothold among the people whose religious training had prepared them for the glorious truths of the restoration. In most other communities where the Bible was regarded as a perfect book that needed no revision or additional scriptures or revelations to clarify or explain the mysterious texts in the old scriptures, there would have been far more persecution, indifference, and bitter opposition. The objections to the Mormon philosophy in this regard, which was popular among most Christian denominations, is well expressed in these words:

> One of the objections which the enemies of the Bible have against it is what they call the "contradictions" in it. The Mormons are chief among those who try to show that there are contradictions in the Bible. They say these contradictions show that the book has not been properly translated, and that God favored the world by giving Joseph Smith a better translation.[12]

In most communities at that time it would have been regarded as blasphemy to speak unkindly of the Bible, revise the sacred text, and add to it a few volumes of scripture equally as sacred and valuable. In a later chapter we shall have more to say about the inspired revision of the scriptures and the revelations that were given in connection with that diligent study of the holy scriptures.

---

[12] *The Octographic Review*, September 23, 1913.

Chapter IX

THE REFORMERS BECOME PERSECUTORS

The moment hundreds of the members of the "Campbellite" fold deserted the movement and accepted the "restoration of the ancient order" as an accomplished fact, not an anticipation, their angry leaders began a bitter persecution against the new reform movement that far eclipsed that the Campbells had started a few years before. As the reform movement of John the Baptist had been swallowed up by the ministry of the Master, so the restoration absorbed and engulfed much of the "Campbellite" reformation in Ohio.

"Alexander Campbell never forgave the Mormons," we are assured by Gates and Huribert, "for running off with Rigdon and many others of his flock." His prolific writings were filled with scathing denunciations against the new religion that had gone further in the work of restoration than he ever dreamed of. The younger Campbell considered Rigdon a traitor who had persuaded his new leader to adopt many of the dogmas of the "Disciples" and put them forth as features of the restoration.

This angry reformer read the Book of Mormon carefully and proceeded to inform his members how to put forth the best arguments against it when they contacted the Mormon missionaries. In his *Millennial Harbinger* under date of February 7, 1831, he published his famous article on "Modern Delusions," in which he had written one of the most comprehensive negative appraisals of the book that has ever been written. He and his colleagues made extensive tours over northern Ohio, holding protracted meetings in all the hamlets on the frontier in an effort to turn the tide against the new movement. The brutal persecution that followed must be laid at the feet of the Campbells and their ministers who were enraged at the success of the Mormons in their very strongholds.

Upon hearing of the "defection" of Sidney Rigdon, the venerable Thomas Campbell took to the frontier where he lectured in Mentor, Hiram, Warren, and other villages, persuading his disturbed flock to remain with him and not be carried away by the "Mormonite delusion." His vigorous campaign together with the writings and preaching of his son are said to have saved the day for them, thus preventing a widespread apostasy from their fold.

They argued that the only truths the Mormons had were stolen from them. They were unmindful of the fact that many other reformers had taught for years that the true Gospel was not on the earth. The historian Mosheim had written of this glorious expectation:

> Some of this class of people, perceiving that such a church as they had formed an idea of would never be established by human means, indulged the hope that God himself would in his own time erect for himself a new church, free from every blemish and impurity; and that he would raise up certain persons, and fill them with heavenly light for the accomplishment of this great object.[1]

In 1534 the brave reformer Rothmann published a book in which he declared: "The world has fallen from the truth, and that it has been misled by the papacy and by the so-called Evangelical teachers, but the time is at hand when Christ shall restore the

---

[1] J. L. Mosheim, *Ecclesiastical History*, Book 4. p. 200.

world lost in sin, and this restoration or restitution of the world shall take place by means of the lowly and unlearned."[2]

It is a well known fact that Roger Williams resigned as pastor over the largest Baptist church in America because "There was no regularly constituted church on earth nor any person authorized to administer church ordinances, nor can there be until new apostles are sent by the Great Head of the Church for whose coming I am seeking."[3]

One of Roger William's biographers wrote that he "denied that any ministry now exists which is authorized to preach the gospel to the impenitent, or to adminster the ordinances."[4] Another biographer wrote that "He considered the church of Christ so fallen in apostasy as to have lost both its right form and the due administration of the ordinances, which could only be restored by some new apostolic or specially commissioned messenger from above.[5]

In 1713 a daring reformer had said:

> Christianity, having degenerated into a Beast and Harlot, receives sentence of condemnation, which yet God is pleased not to execute without calling men to repentance by one more, and that the last Dispensation of his Grace ... In the world's sixth, which is its old age, it shall by the favor of Jesus Christ receive one more Dispensation of his Grace, which will be the last the wicked world is ever to expect. It will consist, as the former did, in appearing, revelation and re-establishment of some ordinances.[6]

The "Campbellites" Condemn Sidney Rigdon

"Fits of melancholy followed by fits of enthusiasm accompanied

---

[2] B. B. Bax, *Rise and P411 of the Anabaptists*, p. 63.
[3] *Picturesque America*, p. 502.
[4] *Cramp's Baptist History*, p. 461.
[5] *Struggles and Triumphs of Religious Liberty*, p. 238.
[6] Peter Poiret, *Economy of the Restoration of Man*, IV, 205.

by some kind of nervous spasms and swoonings which he has since his defection," argued Alexander Campbell, "he interpreted into the agency of the Holy Ghost. . . Baptism for the remission of sins is a phrase not found in their book. A few of their leaders took it from Rigdon . . . The Mormonite religion was got up to deceive the people and obtain their property, and was a wicked contrivance with Sidney Rigdon and Joseph Smith, Jr. May God have mercy on the wicked men, and may they repent of this their wickedness."[7]

The persecution that was thrust upon the Church leaders in Ohio was due almost entirely to the "Campbellite" leaders whose jealous anger knew no bounds. We have wandered far a-field from our appointed task in order to present the complete historical background of the early incidents in Church history and the revelations that were given soon after Joseph Smith arrived in Ohio.

In later chapters we shall see that this extensive and apparently extraneous historical material makes a positive contribution to the early revelations that were given in Ohio. This feature of history has never been presented in its fullness before, yet it was certainly a work of preparation that should not be overlooked.

---

[7] *The Millennial Harbinger*, I, 38.

Chapter X

THE LAND OF SHINEHAH

In the early revelations given in Ohio, Kirtland was often referred to as the land of Shinehah.[1] At that time some of the revelations were printed in the Church publications or announced from the pulpit. At first there was no attempt to conceal or camouflage the message. As a result, the enemy was on hand to attempt to prevent the fulfillment of the prophecy or hinder the execution of the command. For this reason many of the revelations were given in a sort of code, thus concealing from the world the full import of the sacred message. In such revelations Kirtland was called the land of Shinehah.

The Prophet had been in Kirtland but a few days when an important revelation was given.[2] There were, about one hundred members in the young branch at that time, more converts than there were in New York and Pennsylvania where extensive missionary work had been done. Again the revision of the scriptures was emphasized, and plans were soon made for devoting much time to that project.

Communistic Societies

On this restless frontier there were many sects teaching revolution-

---

[1] Doctrine and Covenants 82:12.
[2] Doctrine and Covenants, Section 41.

ary doctrines that could not have got a foothold in the eastern cities where the old, orthodox patterns of religion were so firmly established. One sect at Kirtland had a negro leader called "Black Pete," who received "revelations" for his flock. He even convinced his disciples that he received "letters from heaven." Wycom Clark, another "revelator," had organized "The Pure Church." Referring to such religious groups, the Prophet recorded that "some strange notions and false spirits had crept in" among the members. Among the "strange notions" so popular on the Western Reserve was the communistic society.

Isaac Morely was a leader in one of these societies which was called the "Family" or the "Morely Family," since their communal home was located on his farm. The "Shakers" and other groups in that region were experimenting in this field. The most popular social experiments in this field are briefly summarized as follows:

> *Labadist Commonity.*—Founded in 1694 in Maryland. Jean de la Badie, at first a Jesuit, but later professor on the Reformed Church of France, left that body and a separate church about 1666 near London, advocating a reformation of the Reformed Churches, the ancient gifts of the Holy Spirit, a community of goods, and that all disciples should live and eat together. A settlement was also formed in New York, apparently prior to that in Maryland.[3]
>
> *Order of The Solitary*, sometimes called the *Ephrata Society.*—It was founded in 1732, by Johann Conrad Beissel, at Ephrata, Pennsylvania. Celibacy was approved, but not, enforced. Property was held in commons as a rule, but private ownership was permitted. It grew to about three hundred members, but declined near the time of the Revolution. Some were highly educated, one member, Peter Miller, hav-

---

[3] *Encyclopedia Britannica*, XVI, 16, 2; *Encyclopedia of Social Reform*, pp. 264, 267.

ing translated the Declaration of Independence into seven languages, at the request of Congress.[4]

Shakers; or United Society of Believers.—In 1787 a society was established near Watervliet, New York, on a communistic basis, and grew to seventeen communities with about four thousand members by 1887, but were estimated at five hundred in 1915. The state of celibacy was favored, but not enforced. Private property was regarded as a sin, and affairs were managed by a council.[5]

Harmonists.—About seven hundred and fifty persons under the leadership of John George Rapp, embracing a hundred and forty families in 1805, entered into articles of association on five thousand acres in Butler County, Pennsylvania. Their agreement was "each for all and all for each in sickness and in health." Two years later celibacy began to be the custom. Commercial reasons caused them to move to Indiana, on the Wabash River, in 1814, where thirty thousand acres and the town of New Harmony comprised their property. Being abolitionists, the unfriendly neighbors and commercial reasons caused them to sell out to Robert Owen, and to move to Ohio River near Pittsburgh in 1824. Here they became very prosperous, until division in their ranks, in 1832, caused a division, since which it gradually declined, and was dissolved in 1906.[6]

Zoar Community; also called *Separatists*.—A colony of Germans, numbering about four hundred members, was aided by the Quakers to settle in Tuscarawas County, Ohio, in 1817. In 1819 they adopted articles of agreement for a community of goods, and in 1832 had grown to about five hundred members. In 1885 they had seven thousand acres of land and a million dollars worth of property, their prosperity being

---

[4] *New International Encyclopedia*, VIII, 15.
[5] *International Encyclopedia*, XX, 772. *Encyclopedia Britannica*, XIV, 771.
[6] *New International Encyclopedia*, X, 706, 707.

mostly due to the ability of Joseph Michael Baumeler, a leader, prior to 1837, the time of his death. In 1898 the decline of the society caused them to make a distribution of the property, though as a municipal corporation it remains.[7]

Robert Owen Society.—Several colonies in Great Britain had been formed by Mr. Owen before coming to America in 1824, These not proving successful, he purchased the New Harmony property of the Harmonist Society, but after two years of effort it proved to be unsuccessful also. He advocated the subordination of machinery to man labor, and the bringing up of all children by the community after they became three years of age. Other experiments in Great Britain about the year 1831 were for a time fairly successful. His opposition to prevailing religions caused much trouble with his efforts. The community at New Harmony numbered over a thousand within six months after it was purchased by Owen, but none of the various constitutions adopted proved to be acceptable, and at least ten groups left the society and formed others, because of religious differences.[8]

Perfectionists; later became the *Oneida Community.*—John Humphrey Noyes entered into a contract with followers at Putney, Vermont, in 1843, and the formal association of Perfectionists was formed two years later. The teachings promulgated caused indignation meetings in the village, and in 1847 the society removed to land purchased near Oneida, New York. A member, Mr. Newhouse, invented a steel trap, the manufacture of which was profitable to the community. The doctrine of living together as one family, involved a system of "complex marriage," which so aroused that section of the country that it had to be abandoned. All possessions were held in common until voluntary dissolution took place in 1881, and a joint-stock company was formed to take over the

---

[7] *New International Encyclopedia*, XXIII, 865.
[8] *Encyclopedia Britannica*, XX, 394-396,
New International Encyclopedia, XVII, 650.

property. At that time there were about 238 members, and a branch society of forty-five members at Wallingford, Connecticut. It held six hundred and fifty acres of land, and about six hundred thousand dollars worth of property.[9]

Amana; formerly the *True Inspiration Society.*—Founded at Amana, Iowa, in 1855, going there from Ebenezer, near Buffalo, New York. The Inspirationists are said to have grown out of a sect formed by J. F. Rock in Germany in 1714. Community of goods began to be advocated in 1842, when they moved to America, and in 1843 settled at Ebenezer, where the remained ten years, thence removing to Amana, where they secured land on both sides of the Iowa River. Their constitution declares, "That the land purchased here, and that may hereafter be purchased, shall be and remain a common estate and property, with all improvements thereupon and all appurtenances thereto, as also with all the labors, cares, troubles and burdens, of which each member shall bear his allotted share with a willing heart."

The society now occupies seven villages, twenty-six thousand acres of land, numbers about one thousand eight hundred persons; being approximately one half of all the communists found in the United States. They hold that communism is 'but the outgrowth of their religious life, which is characterized by a belief in continued inspiration. There is no crime, and no poverty among them.[10]

Fourieristic Societies.—These were the outgrowth of doctrines set forth by Charles Fourier. He claimed that on discovering universal laws and applying them, man can become perfect, which will insure social harmony and happiness. His system was based upon the idea that there are twelve passions, of which seeing, feeling, hearing, smelling, and tasting are sensi-

---

[9] *Encyclopedia Britannica*, XX, 106; *New International Encyclopedia*, XVII 457; XVIII.
[10] *New International Encyclopedia*, I, 495; *Encyclopedia Britannica*, I, 779-780; *Harper's Monthly*, CV, 659-688, October, 1902, pp. 659-688.

tive; amity, love, paternity, and ambition are affective; and three, cabalistic, alternating, and composite are distributive. To permit all these passions to have proper expression, the unit society should contain two thousand persons, called a phalanx. Members of a phalanx are to be arranged in groups according to the law governing passional attraction. Each person works where his talents call him, and may change occupations as he desires, making work a pleasure. A minimum is received for labor, and the surplus is distributed in the proportion of five parts to labor, four to capital, and three to talent. I the phalanx was to be ruled by a unarch, a union, of several phalanxes, was to be ruled by *aduarch*, and so on, until the whole Nation and finally the world should be organized.

Albert Brisbane introduced this system into the United States in 1842. It spread with great rapidity, until nearly forty associations were formed, based more or less on the Fourier principle. Horace Greeley advocated it in the *New York Tribune*, and Charles A. Dana also favored it. The phalanx in Monmouth County, New Jersey, lasted twelve years being formed in 1843. The Brook Farm Association, which had been a communistic experiment of which Hawthorne, Dwight, Emerson, Thoreau, and others were members, began in 1841. In 1844 it was reorganized into a Fourieristic community, but in 1847 it was dissolved. Hawthorne's Blythedale Romance utilizes his Brook Farm experiences. Most of these associations survived only a few years.[11]

Cabet Societies; the Icarians.—Cabet espoused communism under the influence of Owen, and proclaimed that Christ came to establish social equality. He established a community in Texas, in 1848, which returned before the end of the year to New Orleans. Hearing that the Mormons had left Nauvoo, he proceeded to that place with about three followers, remaining there, fairly prosperous, till Cabet withdrew, in 1856, from his

---

[11] *New International Encyclopedia*, IX, 101, 102; IV, 17.

society together with those who supported him. In 1860 the Icarians left Nauvoo, which they had entered about the year 1851, and settled in western Iowa, where they prospered until a division took place in 1880, one faction dissolving and the other continuing there until the society dissolved in 1895.[12]

It is significant that Sidney Rigdon had long been in favor of adopting the social order of "all things in common" as a part of the restoration of the ancient order of things. He had labored with Alexander Campbell so much, trying to persuade him to adopt the system that the leader became very angry at Rigdon and ordered him to discuss the subject no more.[13]

Moore insists that he "began to lose caste with the Disciples by seeking to introduce a common property scheme which he declared was a part of the ancient Gospel." Rigdon was severely criticized for trying to thrust this plan upon his leader and master. Failing in this he looked with a sympathetic eye upon the "Family" which was in operation on Isaac Morley's farm, the united order of the Shakers, and other forms of the ancient system of all things in common that were in operation in northern Ohio.

It is significant that the second revelation given in Ohio instituted the law of consecration and made provision for the poor and needy.[14] With the assistance of Rigdon, Isaac Morley, Lyman Wight, Titus Billings, and others who were deeply interested in this practice, the plan soon met with the approval of the new converts.

One new convert, Leman Copley, offered a tract of land in the village of Thompson where the new social experiment could be put in operation. In the spring time when the New York Saints migrated to Ohio, the Colesville branch settled on the welcome

---

[12] *New International Encyclopedia*, IV, 261, 262; XI, 720; *Encyclopedia Britannica*, IV.
[13] Hayden, *op. cit.*, p. 197.
[14] Doctrine and Covenants, Section 42.

tract at Thompson, not far from "Morley's Family," and the system of stewardship was instituted.

In a short time Copley and several of his friends left the Church and his generous offer was withdrawn. The Colesville Saints were soon on their way to Missouri, where they remained as a united group for a long time.

Under the stewardship plan the distribution of goods and disposition of property were made according to needs and abilities. The man who had been a good farmer received more land than the man who could be expected to spend most of his time as a carpenter for the community and would have but little time to till the soil.

When a person entered the Order he deeded to Bishop Partridge all his property and the Bishop in turn deeded back to him all the property he and his family would need. A poor man received much more than he gave, while a man of considerable wealth was expected to share it with the poorer members of the society.

Titus Billings deeded to the Bishop "sundry articles of furniture, two beds, with extra clothing) farm utensils, two horses, two wagons, two cows, two calves, to the total value of $316.50." These same "sundry articles" were deeded back to him, together with "a piece and parcel of land." The contract declared that Billings had first paid his just debts, and would release all right to "the above described property" if he were called to do so. In case of a heavy influx of poor converts he might be expected to share with them some of the possessions that had been deeded to him.

When a similar distribution was later made, the experienced farmer Billings from the fruitful Chagrin Valley was given $27^1/_2$ acres of land, while Joseph Knight, Jr., a carpenter and joiner, was given less than two acres. His friend Levi Jackman, an expert farmer, received 33 acres of good farming land.

Every contract specified that in case of transgression the, delinquent would lose his standing in the Church and in the Order. It also specified that, "I do bind myself to pay the taxes and also to pay yearly into the said Edward Partridge, bishop, or his successor in office, for the benefit of the Church, all that I shall make or accumulate more than is needful for the support and comfort of myself and family." The Bishop was bound to support the members of the Order in "case of their inability in consequence of infirmity or old age" from the funds that were appropriated for that purpose.

Under this system there was no welcome place for the idler. In the years that followed much was said from the pulpit and through the press to discourage indolence. Even revelations declared that the idlers should not eat the bread of the willing workers or wear the clothing they had not earned. "He that will not work is not a disciple of the Lord," declared the Church newspaper.

This revelation also contains the "law" that had been promised in Fayette, which proved a valuable contribution to the theological pattern of the growing society. It is one of the great documents, making a positive contribution to the doctrinal development of the growing society.

One Inspired Mouthpiece

It was perfectly natural that on the western frontier where there were so many sects getting a strong foothold and so many leaders crying, "Lo, Here!" that the question would arise about the validity of the announcements of Alexander Campbell, the "revelations" of "Black Pete," Wycom Clark, and many others. The third revelation given in Ohio dealt with this necessary subject.[15] This is a masterful discussion of this vital question which has not been understood by many men who have sought to exalt themselves as leaders above the men of God's choice.

The Ohio woods were still resounding with the sermons of the "Campbellites" concerning the end of the world and the great events that were to precede it. People were asking Joseph Smith about the restoration of the ancient order of things, the end of the world, the thousand years of peace, and such subjects that agitated the people on the frontier. It is surprizing how many of the early revelations given in Ohio discussed this popular theme."[16]

It is amazing to read the voluminous literature of the "Campbellites," "Millerites," "Shakers," and others who had been proselyting on the frontier, and see what vague speculations and weird predictions they had made regarding this absorbing subject. Surely the Prophet was flooded with questions about these disturbing topics. Section 45 is one of the greatest revelations ever given to the world on this absorbing subject, and it came at an opportune time where the "restorationists," the "shakers," and the "Millennial Saints" had long been discussing those very issues. Since all those cults differed widely on their interpretations, the discussions created widespread confusion and dissatisfaction.

The Gift of Tongues

On the heels of this message was another one of equal importance on spiritual gifts.[17] This advice was especially timely and necessary, as there were many sects on the frontier insisting that they were exercising the gift of tongues. This divine gift had long been exercised in the Church, but in some localities it became extreme and even spurious.

---

[15] Doctrine and Covenants, Section 43.
[16] Doctrine and Covenants 43:16-28; 45:12-75; 133:21-24.
[17] Doctrine and Covenants, Section 46.

Brigham Young had enjoyed the gift of tongues even before he made the acquaintance of Joseph Smith, often using that gift in the meetings of the Saints, some of whom pronounced it "genuine and from the Lord, and others pronounced it of the devil."[18]

The first time Joseph Smith ever heard the gift of tongues was at a meeting in Kirtland soon after Brigham Young had gone to Ohio. The latter was asked to pray at a meeting. During his prayer he spoke in tongues. At the close of the meeting many of the congregation sought the Prophet's opinion of that gift. They had experienced the spurious gift that was manifested by the sects on the frontier, and some considered as spurious the remarks of Brigham Young.

They were informed that they had witnessed the true gift of tongues, having listened to the "pure Adamic language... It is of God."

Brigham Young continued to enjoy the gift of tongues, as did many of the Saints at that time. On one occasion at a meeting in Kirtland he made a short address in tongues. Another person arose and interpreted his remarks. Among other things it was said that "Mary Ann Angel and Brigham Young. are designed of God for each other."[19] Brigham Young's first wife had passed away in New York. He had two children to care for and certainly needed a companion. Soon after this experience he and Mary Ann Angel were married.

> In many meetings of the Saints the gift of tongues was manifested in singing and speaking. At a conference of the Church in 1833 there was an outpouring of the gifts of the spirit, the Prophet recording, "I spoke to the conference in another tongue, and was followed in the same gift by Brother Zebedee Coltrin, and he by Brother William Smith, after

---

[18] *History of the Church* 1, 297, 409, 422.
[19] *Lives of Our Leaders*, p. 87.

which the Lord poured out His Spirit in a miraculous manner, until all the Elders spake in tongues."[20]

In John Whitmer's "History" we are told that:

> At a conference of the Church in June, 1831, Joseph Smith, Jr., prophesied the day previous that the Man of Sin would be revealed. While the Lord poured out his spirit on his servants, the devil took a notion to make known his powers; he bound Harvey Whitlock and John Murdock so they could not speak, and others were affected; but the Lord showed to brother Joseph, the Seer, the design of the thing; he commanded the devil in the name of Christ, and he departed to our joy and comfort...
>
> The Lord gave a revelation concerning this subject after which the Saints came to an understanding on the subject, and harmony prevailed throughout the Church of God; and the Saints began to learn wisdom and treasures of knowledge which they learned from the word of God, and by experience as they advanced in the way of eternal life...
>
> Before the Prophet came to Kirtland a variety of false spirits were manifested, such as caused jumping, shouting, falling down, etc. Joseph said as soon as he came, "God has sent me here, and the devil must leave here or I will."

The sects on the frontier were plagued with spurious gifts and spirits. Most of their meetings were characterized by "tremblers," "convulsionaries," "merry dancers," "whippers," "shakers," and others who sought a physical outlet for their ardent religious fervor and energy. This was hot to be confused with the true gifts of the Spirit, so this revelation explaining the gifts of the divine Spirit was a timely one.

Adams informs us that:

---

[20] *History of the Church*, 1, 323.

Morality and religion were at a low ebb, or at least the latter was chiefly for lighting within if not without; for vagaries, devious sensations, physical and emotional, almost without number; for the "falling," the "jerking," the "rolling," and the "dancing" exercise to the glory of God. The Pilgrims (1817), led by an inspired prophet, and who made of raggedness and uncleanness a virtue, wearing their clothes unchanged as long as they would hold together; for Dylkes, "the leather, wood God" (1828), who at one Ohio camp meeting, announced himself as the professed Messiah; for Jeminah Wilkinson, "the Universal Friend;" for William Miller and the end of the world, with proper ascension, robes, and for Joseph Smith, Jr., and the Mormon Bible.[21]

The most notorious example of this spurious gift of tongues was in the Hulet Branch. On one occasion it was predicted that the members "would be safe that night from any persecution from the enemy," yet that very night the enemy broke into many homes and whipped several people who had been present at the meeting.[22] When the Prophet's opinion was sought on this subject he advised them that "the devil deceived them and they obtained not the word of the Lord, as they supposed they did, but were deceived and as far as the gift of seeing as held by the Hulet Branch, it is of the devil, saith the Lord God."

In addition to several revelations which discussed this subject, the Prophet often offered good advice on the subject, such as the following:

> Be not so curious about tongues; do not speak in tongues except there be an interpreter present; the ultimate design of tongues is to speak to foreigners, and if persons are very anxious to display their intelligence, let them speak to such in their own tongues. The gifts of God are all useful in their

---

[21] J. Q. Adams, *The Birth of Mormonism*, p. 18.
[22] *The Far West Record*, p. 60.

places, but when they are applied to that which God does not intend, they prove an injury, a snare and a curse instead of a blessing.

Speak not in the gift of tongues without understanding it, or without interpretation. The devil can speak in tongues; the adversary will come with his work; he can tempt all classes; can speak in English or Dutch.

Again it may be asked, how it was that they could speak in tongues if they were of the devil. We would answer that they could be made to speak in another tongue, as well as their own, as they were under the control of that spirit, and the devil can tempt the Hottentot, the Turk, the Jew, or any other nation; and if these men were under the influence of his spirit, they of course could speak Hebrew, Latin, Greek, Italian, Dutch, or any other language that the devil knew.

Discerning Spirits

This revelation emphasized the gift of discerning spirits, a valuable gift to be desired on the frontier where so many manifestations in the name of religion were to be seen. One man visited with the Prophet and insisted that he was a lineal descendant of the and Apostle Matthias, even a reincarnation of the ancient Saint. The Prophet informed him that his doctrine was of the devil and that he was in possession of a wicked and depraved spirit.[23]

Years later the Prophet employed an Indian agent as interpreter. He would speak for a few minutes to the assembled multitude of Indians and the agent would then interpret his speech in their language. The moment the Indians showed resentment and anger at his message it was revealed to him that the agent was telling falsehoods in order to prejudice the red men and turn them

---

[23] *History of the Church*, II, 307.

against him. The Prophet pushed him aside and preached a long, sermon to them, every word of which they understood in their own tongue.

The following May more information was revealed on this important subject.[24] Several of the revelations at this time breathed a warning to many men who were not valiant. Ezra Thayer was advised to "repent of his pride and of his selfishness."[25] Five years later he left the Church, He had contributed $800 toward the building of the temple in Kirtland. He thought the brethren would surely reserve a seat for him, but when he went late and found no reservation for him, he apostatized.

At the same time Lyman Wight was advised to beware, "for Satan desireth to sift him as chaff."[26] After the martyrdom of Joseph and Hyrum Smith, Wight started an apostate faction in Wisconsin and later migrated to Texas where he tried hard to build up his kingdom. Upon his death his faction ceased to exist.

Thomas B. Marsh and many of the brethren received words of warning and advice before the migration to Missouri, that should have been the turning point in their lives, but they did not heed the Lord's word.

At this time a command was given that the talented W. W. Phelps should assist Oliver Cowdery "to do the work of printing, and of selecting and writing books for schools in this church, that little children also may receive instruction before me as is pleasing unto me." And thus there began the intense interest in education for young and old that has characterized the Latter-day Saints from that moment.

For several months Oliver Cowdery, Sidney Rigdon, and John Whitmer had served as secretary and recorder, having written the important incidents and revelations. In March, 1831, it

---

[24] Doctrine and Covenants, Section 52.
[25] Doctrine and Covenants 56:8.
[26] Doctrine and Covenants 52:12.

was made known that John Whitmer should be appointed custodian of the records of the Church, Oliver Cowdery having been appointed to another task.[27]

In June, 1831, the Prophet departed from Kirtland, in company with several of the brethren, for the land of Missouri. Several of the last revelations given in Ohio contained information about the proposed journey to "the land of Zion." He had been in Ohio nearly six months, during which time he had received sixteen revelations that, are preserved in the Doctrine and Covenants. The next six were given in Missouri, after which the Prophet was back in Ohio again.

Before considering the revelations that were given in Missouri we must tell the story of the "Shaking Quakers" and discuss the revelation that was given concerning them.

---

[27] Doctrine and Covenants, Section 47.

Chapter XI

THE SHAKING QUAKERS

One of the strangest sects on the frontier was the one known as the Shaking Quakers, or Shakers as they were commonly known. In the spring of 1831 one of their members joined the Church. His name was Leman Copley. He liked the new religion so well that he wanted to go on a mission among his people and tell them of the glorious truths that had been revealed. He wanted to take as his missionary companions Parley P. Pratt and Sidney Rigdon. These men were well acquainted with the teachings of this strange sect and were reluctant to go among them until they were authorized by the Prophet to take the message to them, Before considering the revelation that was given concerning the missionary tour among them, we must tell the story of the Shakers and their peculiar social and theological order. Without that information this revelation is rather meaningless.

This strange sect was started in England in 1747 by James Wardley. The struggling society gained a real convert when Ann Lee accepted the reform Quaker movement of Wardley. From the beginning shaking was the main form of worship for the members of this sect. George Fox had said that people. should tremble at the word of God, so these people developed that form of expression for the religious frenzy they possessed. Ann Lee soon developed the art of trembling so well, that she attracted the attention of many who were in favor of such sensationalism and emotionalism. She could clench her fists so hard that blood was forced through the pores of the skin.

"The work God has designed for the last days," this nervous woman once remarked, "is a work of shaking. The prophets have decreed it." She insisted that she was the woman spoken of in the Apocalypse "clothed in the sun, and the moon under her feet."

At an early age she rebelled against marriage. She shuddered at the thought of swearing allegiance to any man, yet her father demanded that she marry a blacksmith named Abraham Stanley. The more children that came to this union the more she rebelled against marriage. Her first four children died soon after birth. She regarded this as a retribution for having entered the undesirable bond of marriage. She deserted her husband and was put in prison for the offense. The warden was ordered to starve her to death, but a boy she had adopted came to the prison each night, pushed the long stem of a pipe through the key hole in her cell door, and slowly poured milk into the large bowl of the pipe.

During her long confinement she had ample time to think of the glories of the celibate state. The prison officials became alarmed because she could not be starved to death, believing that she was bewitched. They offered her a release from jail if she would leave the country at once. This was what she had long expected. In 1774 she was in America where she soon built up a strong following on the frontier.

She insisted that she was to be called "Mother Ann," since she was Jesus reincarnate in a female form. She was also called the "elect Lady," by her followers. By 1830 they had established many branches on the frontier, being well represented in northern Ohio.

In America she appointed the "sacred dance, the fantastic song, shivering, swooning, falling down," and other physical manifestations as acts of devotion. This hysterical exercise appealed to many of the Pentecostal sects on the frontier, where "jumpers," "barkers," "mutterers," "rollers," and other gymnastic sects abounded.

When converts joined the Shaker family or community they deeded their property to the society, and then "shared the common blessings of the group." If members ever left the group no money or property was given to them. When married couples joined the Shakers they were given a bill of divorcement and were never allowed to associate together again, except in their public dances and worship. Since no children were born in Shaker communities, their only means of growth in membership was through conversion.

In case young children came into the organization with their parents and later chose to live a normal life they were thrust from the society without any financial or property settlement.

In the Shaker settlements the men raised hogs, chickens and cattle, all of which they sold to others, since they never ate flesh at any time. In their large houses the men slept upstairs and the women downstairs. The men and women were allowed to dine in the same room, but were seated at separate tables and were never permitted to speak to one another, lest it lead to levity and romance. They knelt in prayer at the beginning of each meal and bowed in thankful worship as the meal was finished.

Though they dined in the same room they had separate entrances and stairways. In the fields and in the large houses every precaution was taken to keep the sexes separated, yet when they met in their worship it became a frenzied scene of dancing and shaking, though each one performed alone. No couples danced together and nothing was done to attract the attention or admiration of the opposite sex, except as exercises of religious devotion.

It is surprising that dancing became such a popular feature of their religious activity, since they allowed no spirit of levity or romance to creep into their meetings to mar the "dignity" of their worship. Their meetings resembled a gymnasium more than they did an orthodox worship service.

"Mother Ann" offered this advice to the men and women who were never allowed to speak to one another in their houses:

> Why should the tongue, which is the most unruly member of the body, be the only chosen instrument to worship God? God has also created the hands and the feet and enabled them to perform their functions in the service of the body. Shall these important faculties... be active in man's service, or in the service of sin, and yet be idle in the, service of God. Go forth, disciples of Mother Ann, praise God with the members of your bodies!

In their solemn worship service, after a prayer and a song or a short sermon, the benches were pushed against the walls and the shaking and trembling program commenced. Many witnesses have left accounts of their services. Some of the congregation would begin singing, each one his own tune, some without tunes, some without words. Some sang jig tunes in an unknown tongue which they called the gift of tongues. While some were dancing an emotionless square dance, or others were laughing heartily and loudly; others were drumming the floor with their feet, as a few were hissing and chasing the evil spirits from the room. This groaning, jumping, trembling, muttering, and dancing made a bedlam of confusion. In the corners could be seen a few people whirling on their heels in a circle, each one dancing alone and unmindful of any associates. They would whirl as fast and as long as they could remain upon their feet. Some were known to whirl in that manner for more than two hours without resting.

At other times the whole congregation would shout with one accord, under the direction of a leader who would tell them what words to shout. When the dancing commenced, the women who were the best whiners, danced into the center of the group, shouting, singing, whirling, shaking, and trembling, and another dance was soon in session.

When the audience tired of the sermon they would commence jerking and bouncing in their seats and the preacher would encourage them to rise and give vent to their feelings. From the many accounts of their meetings that visitors have left, we glean these accounts:

> They meet together in the night and have been heard two miles by the people in the dead of night; sometimes a company of them will run away to a house, get into it, raise a bedlam, wake up all the house and the neighbors round about for a mile. They run about in the woods and elsewhere hooting and tooting like owls...

> During one of their meetings one of the sisters began to rock her body to and fro, at first gently, then in a more violent manner, until two of the sisters, one on each side, supported her else she would have fallen to the floor. She appeared to be wholly unconscious of her surroundings, and to be moved by an invisible power. The shaking of the subject became violent, and it was with great difficulty that she could be restrained from throwing herself forcibly to the floor. Her limbs were rigid, her face took on an ashen hue, her lips moved and she began to speak in a clear distinct voice, every word of which penetrated every pare of the room which was as still as death. Every eye was upon the recipient of the gift; every ear open to catch every word as it fell from her lips. She

spoke of the shortness of life, of the absolute necessity of abandoning the world and its sinful pleasures before it is too late.[1]

Their most important creed declared that Mother Ann was Jesus Christ in a female form, and that the Millennium had started, since the Savior was upon the earth in the body of Ann Lee. An outstanding feature of their society was the communistic order which they called the "family." Each family consisted of from thirty to ninety members.

The doors of their institutions were not open to everyone as a charitable institution. Old people without money were never allowed to join the society. They refused to take oaths in court or participate in public affairs, never voting on any occasion. They were vigorously opposed to war.

Leaves From Old Journals

A study of some of the old Shaker diaries reveals the spirit of their worship and religious philosophy. The following entries are typical:

> November 28, 1840. After the evening meeting we had the privilege of following Christ's example in washing one another's feet.

> Dec. 16, 1841. We had a very good meeting. In meeting about 22 hours. In the evening many of the ancient saints attended our meeting such as Noah, Abraham, Jeremiah, Isaiah, and also some of the ancient sisters, the Virgin Mary and others...

> Elder Grove had a communication given at New Lebanon

---

[1] *Book of All Religions*, pp. 554-560; *What All the World Believes*, pp. 619,625; C. F. Potter, *The Story of Religion*, pp. 495-529.; C. E. Sears, *Gleanings front old Quaker Journals*, p. 33.

concerning Tea, Swine, Meat, all kinds of strong drink, and coffee.

Jan. 19, 1843. Evening reading meeting. Heard communications from the Holy Holy Mother, Christ and Mother Ann, also a roll from Amos,, a Jew that was on the earth in Christ's day. This evening Jacob of old and his twelve sons attended our meeting. Likewise many other good spirits. Lucy Myrick danced a lively song.

Etiquette in the Dining Room

Their *Manual of Good Manners* contained several pages of instructions on the proper behavior in the dining room. They were expected never to look across the room where the members of. the opposite sex were seated, never speaking to them in their homes or in their religious meetings. Characteristic of their instructions are these items:

> Always sit erect at the table. The body should recline a little forward when eating, to avoid dropping victuals on your clothes. Never looks more clownish at the table than to see a person grasp and handle victuals that he does not want.
>
> Never gaze at a person while he is eating, for it looks as though you covet his victuals. It shows low breeding and selfishness to pick out the best of the victuals, or to turn over a piece of meat to look at both sides of it before you take it to eat. Never pocket victuals at the table, it denotes a thievish disposition. Throw nothing under the table. Always pick your bones clean.

Reincarnation

Their theologians explained that the Savior had "reappeared in

Mother Ann's godly life and searching power; in her self denial; in her humiliation; in her willing suffering afflictions and persecutions." They had much to say about Elias "that was to come the second time." They argued that when Elias made his appearance in the days of Jesus, that it was not necessary "for the same flesh and bones, nor the same person to come, in order for Elias to reappear, but another person to come in his power, spirit and gift. And this truly was the case with our loved Mother Ann Lee."

The status of Mother Ann has thus been explained:

> This work and life fell away as predicted, and the world remained without Christ for more than 1200 years, when in! it was revived and exhibited a second time by a woman—and that woman's name was Ann Lee... The second Eve—Ann Lee—was taken from the flesh of the sleeping antichristian body for a helper for the second Adam, Christ Jesus; and she is called the mother of all living the higher spiritual life. Just so the Bridegroom, Jesus, had the bride Ann, ... Abraham and Sarah were types of Jesus and Ann. The two silver trumpets, the two tablets of the Covenant, the two olive trees, the two olive branches, the King and Queen, the son and daughter, etc., all had their accomplishment in Jesus Christ and Ann Lee, the Bridegroom and the Bride of the new creation of God. [2]

The Shakers were pioneers in many lucrative fields of endeavor. They were the first to dry sweet corn for food. They started the raising and vending of garden seeds, and the preparation and marketing of medicinal herbs and roots. They started the broom business. The first buzz saw was manufactured by a Shaker, as were the first cut nails and metallic pens.

---

[2] L. Eads, *Shaker Theology*, p. 101; *A Defense of the Order, Government and Economy of the United Society called Quakers*, p. 26.

The Shaker Philosophy on Biblical Revision

Most of the religious groups in America at that time considered the Bible a sufficient and satisfactory guide to salvation. To millions of people it needed no additional witnesses of companion volumes of scripture to supplement or explain the book that had "withstood the test of ages." Most of the sects and reform movements on the frontier, however, taught that the Bible was poorly translated and many of its texts were ambiguous. Typical of the Shaker philosophy in this regard we quote from one of their orthodox preachers:

> Now it can only be commendable to revise the text of works of standard authority, to eliminate their errors, and to lessen their ambiguity; but however correctly the principle may be applied in regard to productions of the human mind, can it be possible that it should ever be exercised to rectify the Word of God? That must necessarily remain unalterable forever, or else we must change our conception of the Almighty. But how are we to account for this paradoxical preceding of reediting the sacred Word of God? Orthodox creed-makers find themselves in a dilemma, which permits no alternative but to decide upon these two propositions: either the Bible is the Word of God or it is not...

> Is it rational to believe that God would speak in ambiguous and doubtful phrases when everything depended upon their being correctly understood? And even admitting for the moment the original inspiration, that would soon lose its value, except it continued to inspire succeeding translators and copyists; and more than inspiration would be necessary to protect the scriptures from wilful interpolations and designing fabrications, which are well known to have taken place in many instances. Incorrect translations have led to some ludicrous results. The statue of Moses, to quote a case in point, which is one of the sublimest creations of Michael

Angelo's genius, is adorned with two horns, which fact has greatly puzzled art critics and other inquirers, till it has lately been discovered that the Vulgate, which was the version he consulted, has it that when Moses came down from the mount, after his interview with the Lord, he wore two horns; King James Bible has the more probable account that "his face shone."[3]

Shall We Take the Gospel to the Shakers?

The leaders of the Church were well acquainted with the beliefs and customs of the Shakers, many of them having attended some of their meetings. It is perfectly natural that Elders Rigdon and Pratt would be reluctant to go among them as missionaries without first seeking the Prophet's advice on the matter. When these two missionaries and Leman Copley sought his opinion he likely was not sure of the best method of procedure, so inquired of the Lord. The revelation that was received in answer to his prayer instructed them on matters of doctrine which, without a knowledge of the religious philosophy of the Shakers, seems quite meaningless.[4]

While the Shakers denied the need of baptism, it was made clear that they should be taught to "repent and be baptized." In behalf of the Shakers this great truth was revealed "that whoso forbiddeth to marry is not ordained of God, for marriage is ordained of God unto man." The celibate Shakers would certainly resent this inspired advice concerning marriage, but these facts were to be presented to them nevertheless. After Leman Copley joined the Church he is said to have been "still retaining the idea that the Shakers were right in some particulars of their faith."[5]

---

[3] *The Shaker Manifesto*, p. 127.
[4] Doctrine and Covenants, Section 49.
[5] *History of the Church*, 1, 167.

In this important document it was made clear that Ann Lee was not the Savior incarnate, and that the Millennium had not started. For the vegetarian Shakers it was declared that, "the beasts of the field and the fowls of the air" were ordained for the use of man for food and raiment. It was emphasized that man should not abstain from the use of flesh for food, yet they were cautioned not to shed blood or waste flesh needlessly.

The three missionaries were sure to meet a rebuff from the Shakers when they should declare the new message to them "that the Son of Man cometh not in the form of a woman, neither of a man traveling on the earth." The next verse certainly speaks the language of the Shakers, yet it failed to make an impression on them. It predicted that "the heavens to be shaken, and the earth to tremble and reel to and fro as a drunken man."

In this revelation it was explained that "Zion shall flourish upon the hills and rejoice upon the mountains." This is the second time such a reference was made in the revelations to the destiny of the Church in the mountains. Months before it had been said that "Zion shall rejoice upon the hills."[6]

The three missionaries likely studied this message very carefully, perhaps having a copy of it made for themselves to read and rehearse as they traveled to the Shaker community near Cleveland. A few days later, however, they were back in Kirtland, their mission to the Shakers being a failure. Elder Pratt reported that they "utterly refused to hear or obey the Gospel."[7] The historian John Whitmer recorded that "the Shakers hearkened not to their words and received not the Gospel at that time; for they are bound in tradition and priestcraft, and thus they are led away with foolish and vain imaginations."

People who had grown up in such a peculiar society would be reluctant to listen to the truth, though it had been declared from

---

[6] Doctrine and Covenants 35:24.
[7] *Autobiography of Parley P. Pratt*, (first editions) p. 65.

the heavens for their special benefit. In fact, Leman Copley found it rather impossible to accept all the teachings of the restoration because of the religious pattern he was familiar with for years. He soon drifted from the Church and returned to the Shaker "family," where he remained for a few years. On April 1, 1836, he testified falsely against Joseph Smith in a suit that had been brought against Dr. Philastus Hurlbut who had threatened the Prophet's life.

Since the Shakers were opposed to taking part in any public affairs and especially taking an oath in court, they expelled Copley from their society. He then visited the Prophet, explaining that he had been misinformed, having given a false testimony unknowingly. The tender hearted Prophet readily forgave him and permitted him to be baptized and return to the Church.

It has been said that after Martin Harris left the Church he joined a Shaker community for a year or two.[8]

A few weeks after the martyrdom of Joseph and Hyrum Smith, Brigham Young made a reference to the Shakers in his historic speech that prevented Sidney Rigdon from leading away a large following. "I do not care who leads this Church," he declared, "even though it were Ann Lee; but one thing I must know, and that is what God says about it."

At the present time there is not a Shaker community in operation. A few members, almost one hundred years old are still alive. When these few remnants pass away the Shakers will have passed from the earth, yet down through the years rings that divine message that "marriage is ordained of God and whoso forbiddeth to marry is not ordained of God."

In 1890 there were only fifteen Shaker communities in the United States, with 1,728 members and church property valued at $36,800. This was a decrease in membership of 687 since 1875. In

---

[8] *The Millennial Star*, VIII, 124.

a Shaker graveyard near Boston, Massachusetts there are 310 graves; 136 of the Shakers buried there died under seventy years of age; 174 over seventy, while many lived more than ninety years, and a few over one hundred years.

Though a majority of them lived past the alloted time of three score and ten years, they did not live long enough or enjoy enough prosperity to keep their society alive and spreading into every civilized nation of the earth as the Church has that sent its three missionaries to take the truth to the Shakers. As the last of their members shall soon fall asleep in death, that divine message still rings in our ears that "marriage is ordained of God," and that the Savior will not return to the earth in the form of a woman.

This great revelation, like all others, came in answer to prayer at a particular time to meet a specific need.

Chapter XII

"ASK AND YE SHALL RECEIVE"

In several of the early revelations men were admonished to ask for divine assistance, and they were promised that they should receive the coveted blessing if they asked in faith. The Prophet obeyed this advice and found many opportunities to call upon the Lord in times of crisis or emergency. Especially during the early years of his ministry he found this divine source an abundant fountain filled with the water of life. During his first journey to Missouri he found many perplexing problems that could not have been solved except by means of divine wisdom from heaven.

The Land of Zion

The four missionaries to the Lamanites had opened the portals and blazed the trail to Independence, Missouri-the rendezvous of destiny. In the early summer of 1831 Joseph Smith and a few friends made the long journey to the border of the Lamanites. Though they were approaching sacred soil they were doing so at a very critical time. For a decade there had been a wild, lawless element on the Missouri frontier. Since the Missouri Compromise in 1820 the settlers there had been opposed to an influx of settlers from the North. During the years that the Saints tried to establish a foothold in the land of Zion they were the victims of political as well as religious persecution. It was a time when passions were influenced by the struggle of the pro and anti-slavery forces over the Missouri question. As late a May 7, 1836, Daniel Webster wrote of the situation in Missouri, "We are in a peck of trouble here, and I hardly see our way through."[1]

Soon after the Prophet arrived in Zion he received several important revelations.[2] The history of this period is so well known that one should read the revelations that were given at the time, catching the spirit and atmosphere of the occasion.

A wealth of information was revealed during the brief visit in Zion. The land of Zion was dedicated as a gathering place, the site for the temple was dedicated, and the ministry in that historic land was launched in a blaze of divine communications. In a short time the Saints purchased many acres of choice land in that fertile area. Their contributions were placed in the hands of Bishop Edward Partridge who soon purchased 1,985 acres in Jackson County. More than half bf that land lay within the present confines of Kansas City, including such valuable property as the Martha Slavens Memorial Church, the sixty acre tract which includes the Country Club Plaza, Elmsdale, and Bismark Place. A southwest quarter section includes Westwood Park, Vogel Park, Waverly Place, and a quarter section in the beautiful Sunset Hill area.

The Country Club Golf Links, Rockhill Place, Brookside Boulevard, Crestwood and Southwood Parks, and other valuable properties are now located where the Saints purchased their first tracts of land in Zion.

The mission in Zion being completed, the Prophet and a few of his friends were on their way back to Kirtland. During the return journey two important revelations were received, imparting

---

[1] Carl R. Fish, *American Diplomacy*, p. 252.
[2] Doctrine and Covenants, Sections 57, 58, 59, and 60.

valuable information to the Saints.3 They traveled mostly by water, following the rivers and canals as much as they could. At that time there were no railroads on the frontier, but systems of canals stretched from the rivers to distant cities, making it possible to travel extensively by water.

On the third day of their return journey while camped on the shore of the river they heard a "most horrible" sound as the river was churned and troubled by some unseen power. W. W. Phelps saw in open vision the destroyer riding upon the waters. When the Prophet prayed concerning the matter he received the revelation that is preserved in Section 61.

This inspired message stressed the value of missionary work, asserting that "it is not needful for this whole company of mine Elders to be moving swiftly upon the waters, whilst the inhabitants on either side are perishing in unbelief." It asserted that the waters had been cursed in the last days, and advised the Saints to travel by land as much as possible. The destructions upon the waters that were predicted in this revelation have certainly been fulfilled in times of war when torpedoes, mines, and submarines have caused the sinking of hundreds of ships and the loss of thousands of lives.

During the last week in August the Prophet returned to Kirtland. A few days later he received another revelation that was filled with information about the gathering to the land of Zion.4 While preparations were being made for a migration to western Missouri another revelation gave a wealth of information of the subject.5

In September the Prophet, moved to Hiram where he resided in the home of "Father" John Johnson. In that village many valuable revelations were received during the months that he was a guest in the Johnson home.

---

3 Doctrine and Covenants, Sections 61 and 62.

The Publication of the Revelations

In the autumn of 1831 a special conference was held in Hiram to consider the publication of the revelations that had been received up to that time. When it was agreed to publish the revelations in book form, the Prophet received a long revelation that was to serve as a preface or introductory chapter to the volume. This is the reason that the first section in the Doctrine and Covenants was given at the late date of November 1, 1831, while all the revelations following it in the first collection were given before that date. The world will be searched in vain for a more appropriate preface than this great document.

The Most Wise Among You

During this conference most of the members present testified that they knew that the revelations were "of the Lord," but one man was present who objected to the language and literary style in which they were expressed.

He was William E. McLellin, who had taught school successfully in five states of the Union and had acquired a wealth of worldly wisdom. He proposed in a sarcastic attitude of criticism and ridicule that the revelations be rewritten and revised, to go forth to the world in perfect English.

This was a severe rebuke to Joseph Smith and might have been a source of embarrassment, as a few friends of McLellin's and the apostates in that neighborhood were in full sympathy with his philosophy. The Lord answered the challenge, thereby exalting the Prophet in the eyes of his friends and dethroning the "brilliant" McLellin.[6]

The Lord directed that "the most wise among you" should

---

[4] Doctrine and Covenants, Section 63.
[5] Doctrine and Covenants, Section 64.
[6] Doctrine and Covenants, Section 67.

select what was considered the least of the revelations, and try to write one as good as it. If the "wise" individual could write one as good as the weakest one in the collection under consideration, they would not be obliged to accept the ones Joseph Smith had written. McLellin gladly accepted the challenge and wrote a document for the group to consider. Upon reading it they pronounced it a failure, agreeing, that the revelations were certainly "of the Lord." At this same time another revelation was received which is preserved in Section 133.

The Book of Commandments

The members of the Church had long been anxious to have the revelations published in book form so they could own a printed copy. Many of the most important revelations had been multiplied in manuscript form, the missionaries taking copies with them when they went forth to preach. Within three months after the Church was organized the Prophet was compiling the revelations and putting them in suitable form for publication.[7] This was the humble beginning of this modern book of scripture.

At the conference in Hiram the final preparations were made for the collection and publication of these valuable documents. It is significant that the brethren who "prized the revelations to be worth to the Church the riches of the whole earth," planned to publish them to the world in an edition of 10,000 copies. At the present time most of the large publishing houses of the world limit the first edition of their books to 2,500 copies. The leaders of the Church realized that this precious volume deserved such a hearty welcome as to come forth in an edition that large. The Book of Mormon had issued from the press in an edition half that large.

At the close of the conference at Hiram, the Prophet agreed to have all the revelations available by the fifteenth of November,

---

[7] *History of the Church*, 1, 104.

at which time Oliver Cowdery and John Whitmer were expected to be ready to depart for Independence, Missouri, bearing the precious documents that were to be published on the Church press in that place. Joseph Smith dedicated the two messengers and the sacred writings that were entrusted to their care.

In Zion it was a slow and laborious task to set up the type on a small press and print the material that was to constitute the Book of Commandments. As late as June 25, 1833, Sidney Rigdon wrote a long letter to the brethren in Missouri, answering many questions they had asked. His instruction advised them to hasten the publication of the proposed book, omitting the binding of the books since that would keep the books too long from circulation." The same letter called attention to a few typographical errors that should be corrected, and mentioned some "revelations received within a short time back, which you will obtain in due season."[8]

During the Prophet's visit to Missouri it was agreed that the first edition should be limited to 3,000 copies, perhaps as a means of hastening its publication. It was also agreed that Emma Smith's collection of hymns should be published at the same time.

As the project was nearing completion, a letter from the First Presidency in Kirtland advised the brethren in Missouri to "Consign the box of the Book of Commandments to Newel K. Whitney and Co., Kirtland, Ohio." This long-awaited shipment was never made. On July 20, 1833, a mob broke into the printing office, destroyed the paper and publications, seized materials of value, and razed the building to the ground.

It is said that one of the brethren employed in the office at the time the enemy broke into the shop, seized an armful of the printed sheets, ran out the back door and buried them in a pile of straw in an old barn. These few smuggled copies of the incomplete book were the only copies preserved. They were later recovered and dis-

---

[8] Ibid., I, 362.

tributed among the leaders of the Church who had them bound for their own use.

Five folds of the book were set up in type and printed before the press was destroyed. The printed matter consisted of 127 pages, the last fold ending with verse 36 of Section 64, the last words being these, "the rebellious are not of the blood of Ephraim." On February 13, 1833 the title page of the Book of Commandments was filed with the clerk of the United States district court, with the understanding that copies of the book would be filed when it came from the press.

The last Section in the volume was revealed September 11, 1831. If all the revelations that were received up to the time that the press was destroyed had been included in the first edition, it would have included the first ninety-six sections together with Section 133. Some of the ones received between these dates had already been published in *The Evening and Morning Star*. The Appendix, which now is preserved in Section 133, was not published in the Book of Commandments, though it was revealed November 3, 1831.

It is not clear why the name "Appendix" was applied to this revelation and why that title has continued through the years. It is not unlikely that the reason is this: it was revealed just two days after the Preface was given. Since it was the most recent revelation up to that time and since the brethren expected to print the volume immediately, they expected to place it at the close of the volume and thus called it the "Appendix." The Book of Commandments was never finished, so this important chapter was not printed in the incomplete edition that was preserved. However, it was printed at the end of the Doctrine and Covenants in 1835 and has served as a fitting climax to the collection of revelations. It was followed by the article on Governments and Laws in General, which is reserved in Section 134, and the account of the martyrdom of Joseph and Hyrum Smith, which is preserved in Section 135, and the last Section in the volume which was given to President Brigham Young.

The few copies of this incomplete volume that were smuggled into the barn and concealed in a pile of straw are the rarest and most expensive of any of the publications of the Church. The author knows of only about twelve copies in existence today. While the Palmyra edition of the Book of Mormon is worth $35.00 to most collectors, the rare Book of Commandments would bring a fabulous price from eager collectors.

The Doctrine and Covenants

After the Saints were expelled from Jackson County, Missouri, the publishing plant was transferred to Kirkland. In the autumn of 1834 the brethren were again considering the problem of printing the revelations. Joseph Smith, Oliver Cowdery, Sidney Rigdon, and Frederick G. Williams were appointed to prepare the material and supervise its publication. This volume was to be known as the Doctrine and Covenants. A year later they had completed their work, and a general assembly was called to accept this volume of sacred scripture.

In 1835 the Doctrine and Covenants issued from the press. In addition to the revelations, it contained the "Lectures on Faith," an article on Government and Laws in General, which now appears in Section 134, and an article on Marriage, which is not included in later editions of the volume. These lectures and the two articles were not received as doctrine on an equal basis with the revelations.

The 1835 edition comprised 257 pages, the seven Lectures on Faith occupying 69 pages. There were few verse divisions in the first edition, which with the small type did not make as pleasing and inviting pages as do the later editions. The chapters were not broken up into as many verse divisions as they are in later editions. The Preface had only eight verses, whereas in the present edition it is broken into thirty-nine verses. The second chapter in the 1835 edition is Section 20 in the present edition. It contained only twenty-seven verses in the first edition, while the present one breaks into eighty-four verses.

It is significant that in the first edition the first three verses of the Word of Wisdom were set in italics and served as a superscription or introduction. The first verse commenced with the line, "Behold, verily thus saith the Lord unto you."

Five years after the Book of Mormon came , from the press another volume of sacred writings was published to the world.

The Pearl of Great Price

The Pearl of Great Price was first published in Liverpool, England in 1851. In addition to what is included in the present edition it included "a Key to the Revelations of St. John," which now comprises Section 77 in the Doctrine and Covenants, and "The Prophecy on War," which is preserved in Section 87. Seven pages of choice selections from the Doctrine and Covenants, and John Jacque's popular poem, "O, Say What is Truth," were included in the first edition of the third book of scripture for this generation.

Persecution in Hiram

In the autumn of 1831 when they were considering the publication of the Book of Commandments in the hamlet of Hiram, there arose a wave of opposition in that community. This had been a busy time for the Church leaders. Four special conferences had been held to consider the publication of the revelations, at which time many revelations had been given, the work of the ministry, the revision of the scriptures, and other pressing duties taxed their energy and time. As soon as it was decided to publish the Book of Commandments and everything was completed for that project, Joseph Smith and Sidney Rigdon were commanded to go forth as missionaries and lift up their voices in opposition to what Ezra Booth and other enemies were saying against them.9

Since so many of the "Campbellites" had joined the Church, their leaders started a vicious persecution in an effort to prevent others from accepting the message of the restoration. With the apostasy of Ezra Booth, Symonds Ryder, and others a tide of opposition was rising against the Church. Its strongest forces were consolidated in the hamlet of Hiram. In a neighboring town Booth was publishing many falsehoods against the Church, attempting to crush the Church to which he had been miraculously converted for a season. Urgent as the work of the ministry was in Hiram, Joseph Smith and Sidney Rigdon were commanded to go forth in the majesty and spirit of their divine calling to "confound your enemies! call upon them to meet you in public and in private. . . let them bring forth their strong reasons against you."

When these stalwart leaders were advised to go forth and "labor in my vineyard for a season," they were assured that "there is no weapon that is formed against you shall prosper; and if any man lift up his voice against you he shall be confounded in mine own due time."

In the following chapter we shall discuss the opposition that abounded in northern Ohio, thus showing the pressing need of this commandment at this critical time. During the passing years the enemy has certainly been confounded. The "Campbellites" then had their strongholds spread over the frontier from Virginia to

---

9 Doctrine and Covenants, Section 71.

Ohio and from New York to Florida, but while the restored Church has spread to every civilized nation of the earth, gathering many disciples from every land under the heavens, the "Campbellite" fold has ceased to grow. Today they have a few organized branches in the land. Their proselyting efforts are aimed largely against the Mormons. They have a college in Texas where they train their ministers in the art of arguing against the "Mormonites" just as Alexander Campbell did in his day.

In 1946 they sent one of their ministers to Europe. He told the author that he intended going into all the large branches of the Church in that land and give them Alexander Campbell's version of the Book of Mormon. The present condition of this struggling society is an example of the confusion that befell them in the due time of the Lord.

Chapter XIII

THE VISION OF GLORIES

After residing in Kirtland for many months, the Prophet and his wife were invited to enjoy the hospitality of John Johnson and his family. In the autumn of 1831 they moved to his home which was in the village of Hiram, about thirty miles from Kirtland. Hiram was a hotbed of "Campbellism," where a few converts had been made. The ones who remained with the "Disciples" were so angry at the Mormons that they were determined to put an end to the movement.

Among the leaders in this persecution were Jacob Scott, Ezra Booth, Symonds Ryder, and others who had joined the Church for a season and had apostatized, becoming vicious and brutal in their designs to thwart the work of the Lord in that community. Joseph Smith was headed for trouble and persecution when he rode home with "father Johnson" to spend the winter in his large frame house.

Ryder had been in the Church but a short time until the Prophet and Sidney Rigdon wrote him a letter, informing him that it was the will of the Lord that he should go on a mission. Since he did not have a strong testimony and was not anxious to become a missionary he objected to the way his name had been spelled. He spelled it Symonds Ryder, whereas it was spelled Symonds Rider in the letter that sought to call him to the ministry. The revelation that mentioned him also misspelled his name.[1] He was thus convinced that the inspiration that resulted in his missionary call was responsible for the spelling of his name-the wisdom of men, not the inspiration of heaven. For this reason he left the Church and became a bitter enemy. The persecutions that soon followed in Hiram were a result of the pernicious activities of Ryder and his angry colleagues.

The winter months were spent in revising the scriptures. There were enough strong leaders in all the branches in northern Ohio by that time so that the Prophet could leave many responsibilities for others, as he devoted all his spare time to an intensive and inspired revision of the scriptures. He had scarcely arrived in Kirkland when he was instructed, "Thou shalt ask, and my scriptures shall be given as I have appointed, and they shall be preserved in safety."[2]

A few days later he was advised to commence the revision of the New Testament, his study up to that time having been concerned with the Old Testament.[3] At this time they turned to Matthew and began to revise that book. For a time they alternated, reading a time from the Old and then turning to the New Testament.

In the Johnson home at Hiram they read many of the books in both testaments, making hundreds of changes in the text. The changes were not confined to grammatical corrections, but lengthy additions were supplied in several places. At the close of Genesis was added the prophecy made by Joseph in Egypt, which was preserved in Nephi.[4]

Hundreds of statements like "the Lord hardened Pharaoh's heart" were changed to read that "Pharaoh hardened his heart."

---

[1] Doctrine and Covenants 57:37.
[2] Doctrine and Covenants 42:56.
[3] Doctrine and Covenants 45:60-61.
[4] II Nephi 3:11-22.

"It repented the Lord that he had created man," is made to read that Noah repented of the fact. Many faulty texts were revised, such as this mysterious text, "Ye shall not eat of anything that dieth of itself: thou shalt give it unto the stranger that is in thy gates, that he may eat it; or thou mayest sell it unto an alien."[5] The inspired revision insists that such flesh should not be eaten, sold or given away.

The disputed text that declares that Melchizedek was "without father, without mother, without descent," is made to read that the priesthood which he held was "after the order of the Son of God which order was without father, without mother, without descent."[6]

As a sample of the hundreds of changes that were made in the text we present a few comparisons:

OLD TESTAMENT

KING JAMES VERSION	INSPIRED VERSION
Genesis 1:1, In the beginning God created the heaven and the earth.	Gen. 1:2, I am the Beginning and the End; the Almighty God. By mine Only Begotten I created these things.
Genesis 1:26, And God said, Let us make man in our image, after our likeness.	Gen. 1:27, and I, God, said unto mine Only Begotten, which was with me from the beginning, Let us make man in our image, after our likeness; and it was so.
Genesis 2:5, And every plant of the field before it was in the earth and every herb of the field before it grew: for the Lord God had not caused it to rain upon the earth, and there was not a man to till the ground.	Gen. 2:4-5,....and every plant of the field before it was in the earth, and every herb of the field before it grew; For I, the Lord God, created all things of which I have spoken, spiritually, before they were naturally upon the face of the earth; for I, the Lord God, had not caused it to rain upon the face of the earth.

---

[5] Deuteronomy 14:21.
[6] Hebrews 7:3.

KING JAMES VERSION	INSPIRED VERSION
Genesis 6:6, And it repented the Lord that he had made man on the earth, and it grieved him at his heart.	Gen. 8:13, And it repented Noah, and his heart was pained, that the Lord made man on the earth, and it grieved him at the heart.
Genesis 22:1, And it tame to pass after these things, that God did tempt Abraham.	Gen. 22:1, And it came to pass after these things, that God did try Abraham.
Exodus 6:27, These are they which spake to Pharaoh, king of Egypt, to bring out the children of Israel from Egypt; these are that Aaron and Moses.	These are they concerning whom the Lord speak to Pharaoh, king of Egypt, that he should let them go. And he sent Moses and Aaron to bring out the children of Israel from Egypt.
Exodus 7:9, Shew a miracle for you.	Show a miracle that I may know you.
Exodus 7:13, And he hardened Pharaoh's heart.	And Pharaoh hardened his heart.
Exodus 22:18, Thou shalt not suffer a witch to live.	Thou shalt not suffer a murderer to live.
Exodus 32:12, Turn from thy fierce wrath and repent of this evil against thy people.	Turn from thy fierce wrath. Thy people will repent of this evil.
Exodus 33:21, And he said, Thou canst not see my face; for there shall no man see me and live.	And he said unto Moses, Thou canst not see my face at this time, lest mine anger be kindled against thee also, and I destroy thee and this people, for there shall no man among them see me at this time, and live, for they are exceeding sinful. And no sinful man hath at any time, neither shall there be any sinful man at any time, that shall see my face and live.
I Samuel 16:14, But the Spirit of the Lord departed from Saul and an evil spirit from the Lord troubled him.	I Sam. 16:14, The Spirit of the Lord departed from Saul, and an evil spirit which was not of the Lord troubled him.

KING JAMES VERSION

II Samuel 19:3, There is no speech nor language where their voice is not heard.

2 Chronicles 18:22, Now therefore, behold the Lord hath put a lying spirit in the mouth of these my prophets.

Psalms 22:12, Many bulls have compassed me: strong bulls of Bashan have beset me.

Psalms 32:1, Blessed is he whose transgression is forgiven, whose sin is covered.

Psalms 42:3, My tears have been my meat day and night, while they continually say unto me, Where ; thy God?

Isaiah 2:9, And the mean man bow, eth down, and the great man humbleth himself: therefore forgiven them not.

Isaiah 8:19, And when they shall say unto you, Seek unto them that have familiar spirits, and unto wizards that peep and that mutter: should not a people seek unto their God? for the living to the dead.

Isaiah 29:10 ...and hath closed your eyes, and the prophets and your rulers the seers hath he covered.

INSPIRED VERSION

No speech nor language can be, if their voice is not heard.

The Lord hath found a lying spirit in the mouth of these thy prophets.

Many armies have compassed me, strong armies of Bashan have beast me around.

Blessed are they whose transgressions are forgiven, and who have no sins to be covered.

My tears have been poured out unto thee day and night, while mine enemies continually say unto me, Where is thy God?

And the mean man boweth not down, and the great man humbleth himself not; therefore forgive him not.

...should not a people seek unto their God? for the living to hear from the dead?

...ye have closed your eyes, and ye have rejected the prophets, and your rulers, and the seers hath he covered because of your iniquities.

NEW TESTAMENT	
INSPIRED VERSION	INSPIRED VERSION
Matthew 5:3, Blessed are the poor in spirit: for theirs is the kingdom of heaven.	Matthew 5:5, Yea, blessed are the poor in spirit, who come unto me; for theirs is the kingdom of heaven.
Matthew 5:6, Blessed are they which do hunger and thirst after righteousness: for they shall be filled.	Matthew 5:8, And blessed are all they that do hunger and thirst after righteousness; for they shall be filled with the Holy Ghost.
Matthew 5:22, But I say unto you, That whosoever is angry with his brother without a cause shall be in danger of the judgment.	Matthew 5:24, But I say unto you, that whosoever is angry with his brother, shall be in danger of his judgment.

The Revised Version omits the words "without cause," as did Joseph Smith, explaining in the notes that "many ancient authorities insert without cause." These words are omitted from all modern translations since they are not found in the oldest and most genuine manuscripts.

Tolstoy, the great Russian scholar, admits that he could never harmonize that statement with the teachings of Jesus, for the Master made no trifling excuses for anger as is conveyed in this sentence. It required but little search among early Greek manuscripts to convince him that these words were not in the original documents.

Matthew 6:13, And lead us not into temptation.	Matthew 6:14, And suffer us not to be led into temptation.
Matthew 6:30, Shall he not much more clothe you, o ye of little faith.	Matthew 6:34. How much more will he not provide for you, if ye are not of little faith.
Matthew 10:16, wise as serpents and harmless as doves.	Matthew 10:16, Wise servants, and harmless as doves.
Mark 6:9, And not put on two coats.	Mark 6:9, And not take two coats.
Mark 10:27, And Jesus looking upon them saith, With men it is impossible, but not with God: for with God all things are possible.	Mark 10:26, And Jesus, looking upon them, said, With men that trust in riches, it is impossible; but not impossible with men who trust in God and leave all for my sake, for with such all these things are possible.

There are 2,995 words added to Mark, and many words changed, yet all of the changes are very superficial. The improvements in Mark are not comparable with those in Matthew.

KING JAMES VERSION	INSPIRED REVISION
Luke 18:27, And he said, The things which are impossible with men are possible with God.	Luke 18:27, And he said unto them, it is impossible for them who trust in riches, to enter into the kingdom of God but he who forsaketh the things which are of this world, it is possible with God, that he should enter in.
John 1; 1, In the Beginning was the Word, and the Word was with God, and the Word was God.	In the beginning was the Gospel preached through the Son. And the Gospel was the word, and the word was with the Son, and the Son was with God, and the Son was of God.
John 1:18, No man hath seen God at any time.	And no man hath seen God at any time, except he hath borne record of the son for except it is through him no man can be saved.
John 2:11, And his disciples believed on him.	And the faith of his disciples was strengthened in him.
John 2:22, they believed the Scriptures.	They remembered the Scriptures.
John 3:32, No man receiveth his testimony.	But few men receive his testimony.
John 4:24, God is a Spirit: and they that worship him must worship him in the spirit and in truth.	John 4:26, For unto such hath God promised his Spirit. And they who worship him, must worship in spirit and in truth.
John 5:29, And shall come forth, they that have done good, unto the resurrection of life and they that have done evil, unto the resurrection of damnation.	And shall come forth they who have done good, in the resurrection of the just and they who have done evil, in the resurrection of the unjust.
John 6:54, I will raise him up at the last day.	I will raise him up in the resurrection of the just.

Dr. P. Marion Simms was very favorably impressed with the change the Prophet made in Matthew 26:26. In the Protestant Bible the Savior is represented as saying, "Take, eat; this is my body." The Douay Version which the Catholics use gives about the same translation. "Take ye, and eat. This is my body." The Inspired Revision gives it this clear meaning, Take, eat; this is in the remembrance of my body which I give a ransom for you.

These few comparisons are typical of the hundreds of changes they made in the text of the Protestant Bible.

The Apocrypha

While this inspired labor was in progress at Hiram, a few revelations were given concerning it that were regarded as valuable enough to be preserved in the Doctrine and Covenants. Section 77 was revealed during this revision of the Apocolypse. A few days later, as the revision was drawing to a close, the Prophet inquired about revising the Apocrypha. This is a collection of seven books that were preserved in the Latin Vulgate, being preserved at the present time in the Bible used by the Catholics. The first editions of the King James Version included these "doubtful" books at the close of the Old Testament instead of keeping them in their natural order as they are retained in the Douay Version.

The Bible that Joseph and Sidney used had the Apocrypha at the close of the Old Testament, so it was perfectly natural that they should be concerned about these books as the revision of the New Testament was completed and only a few books in the Old Testament remained to be revised. The answer to this inquiry is significant. "There are many things contained therein," we learn from a divine source, that are true, and it is mostly translated correctly; there are many things contained therein that are not true, which are interpolations by the hands of men ... It is not needful that it should be translated."[7]

It is significant that for more than two centuries the pulpit editions of the Protestant Bible contained the Apocrypha, as did many editions of the smaller volume, but soon after this revelation was given the Apocrypha began to be omitted from the King James Version. Soon after 1836 the spirit of Elijah was poured out over the whole earth, people everywhere becoming deeply interested in genealogical research. In like manner the Apocrypha fell into disfavor soon after the Lord revealed that "there are many things contained therein that are not true, which are interpolations by the hands of men."

The writer has made a special study of this subject, discovering that the "doubtful" books were popular in the Authorized Version until about 1830, but from that time forward these books were rejected from the Protestant Bible.

The advice to "understand, for the Spirit manifesteth truth," is good advice regarding these books. St. Augustine once said of them:

> This reverence have I learnt to give to those books of Scripture only which are called canonical. Others I so read that I think not anything to be true because they so thought it, but because they were able to persuade me either by those canonical authors, or by some probable reason, that it did not swerve from the truth.

The Three Kingdoms of Glory

During this inspired study of the Bible there must have been a flood of wisdom upon the minds of the students that were not included in the revised text of the Bible. One such document has

---

[7] Doctrine and Covenants. 91:1-6.

been preserved in the Doctrine and Covenants, the great vision of the heavenly kingdoms.[8]

Questions arose in their minds as they considered the text that spoke of the resurrection of the good "to life" and "they that have done evil, unto the resurrection of damnation."[9] Since they did not fully understand this text they prayed for information regarding it. A vision was opened to their minds and they seemed to look into eternity as a voice explained the scenes they were shown.

It was a cold day in winter, February 16, 1832, that the two students prayed for divine information. There were many Saints in the village, some of whom came daily seeking the Prophet's advice on various problems, or to exchange greetings with him. During this vision a few friends walked into the parlor of the Johnson home and stood in sheer bewilderment as they watched and listened. Philo Dibble was one of the witnesses and has left us a description of that wonderful scene.

The two men would stare out in space, oblivious of walls, ceiling, or the few friends who had entered the room unbidden and unnoticed. "I see a glorious kingdom," Joseph would say, "and the voice tells me that this is the church of, the Firstborn. . . "Sidney would nod his head in approval and then remark that the scene had changed and he now saw a lesser kingdom and a voice declared it to be the terrestrial world. "These are they who are of the terrestrial," declared the voice. "And now the scene changes." Joseph interpolated, "and the voice declares this to be the telestial world, and these are they who receive the telestial glory."

Philo Dibble declared that ten or twelve men crowded into the room during the vision, standing there staring at the ceiling as the two men gazed into, the heavens. These visitors did not see any of the miraculous scenes, nor did they hear the voice that explained the various kingdoms that were shown to them. The

---

[8] Doctrine and Covenants, Section 76.
[9] John 5:29.

vision lasted two or three hours, most of which time the visitors stood in the room, yet seemed unnoticed by the two men who were shown the vision.

"What do I see?" was asked many times by these two men, then each in turn would explain what had been shown to him and related what the voice was saying to him. The other always agreed that he saw and heard the same things. This account is preserved in the Juvenile Instructor, volume 27, page 303, and is a valuable contribution to the understanding of the method in which this revelation was received.

And thus the great vision was given. When it was over Sidney was so weak he could scarcely lift a glass of water to his lips. The Prophet remarked that the early visions he received affected him that way, but he was now accustomed to them. This glorious vision was soon recorded exactly as it was given and as it is preserved today. It is one of the greatest revelations ever given to the children of men. It came like all divine messages, in answer to prayer. Not at any time did the Lord thrust a revelation upon His servants. They always came when asked for and when needed most.

In the Camp of the Enemy

Information like this could not be kept a secret in a small community where there were many members to share the good news and many of the enemy to spread it abroad. Often from the pulpit or the press the heaven-inspired truths were announced to the world soon after they were received. Given in the presence of witnesses this remarkable vision was soon being talked about in the community. In a few days it would reach the ears of the jealous "Campbellite" leaders who were getting enraged at the way "the Mormonites were stealing their thunder."

The irate reformers preached against the new doctrines and flooded their publications with tirades against the reformation that was sweeping far ahead of their own reform movement. The *Millennial Harbinger* carried such challenging titles as this, "Mormonism—the means by which it Stole the True Gospel," in an effort to turn the public mind against the popular movement that was sweeping the frontier and seriously reducing the membership in the fold of the "Disciples."

Hiram was the headquarters of the enemy camp. Sidney Rigdon and many of their leaders who united with the true Church had resided there and their characters and works were well known. The "Disciples" who apostatized from the Church—Ezra Booth, Symonds Ryder, Jacob Scott, and others—lived in that village or were well known there. In that hamlet a movement was brewing to drive the Mormons from the village.

The Campbells and their ministers were enraged be, cause Joseph Smith had "adopted" so many of their teachings, followed their advice and began to revise the Bible, and had convinced many people that his message was divine. In fact they insisted that every important thing that the "Mormonites" taught had been borrowed from them. They rebelled against the revision of the Bible which had made such progress in Hiram. The brilliant Campbell had made many revisions in the New Testament which the three ministers had produced in Ireland. Now the unlearned leader of the Mormons was doing far more in his biblical revision than the daring Campbell had done. At this time the enemy was angry enough to drive the Mormons from the town. They were waiting for one more crisis to arise that would kindle the flame that was ready to ignite and cause a great conflagration.

The great vision on the three degress of glory was the issue that brought this hostile movement to a head. This message which was so well received by the Saints, kindled the anger of the enemy until it knew no bounds. This glorious revelation in the wake of an extensive revision of the Bible, brought Alexander Campbell and his father on a lecture tour to save their flock at this time of crisis. At Hiram, Mentor, Mantua, Kirtland, and many other villages their voices were raised in opposition to the new movement.

This revelation on the three heavenly kingdoms was the last straw-the straw that broke the Campbell back. One opponent complained that Joseph Smith "out-masoned King Solomon," but the "Campbellites" complained that he had stolen their thunder and was running wild with it.

Campbell's Three Kingdoms

This incident provoked them to the breaking point because just one year before the Church was organized, Alexander Campbell had expressed his belief in "The Three Kingdoms."[10] If Joseph Smith had ever heard about this doctrine it certainly would not have influenced him in the least in writing the famous document he recorded on the three heavenly kingdoms. Campbell's philosophy is a good example of the wisdom and conjectures of men. His views when contrasted with the revealed will of the Lord seem childish and worldly, yet they were responsible for the collection of a mob with intent to kill Joseph Smith and Sidney Rigdon.

For the purpose of acquainting the reader with the worldly views of Alexander Campbell on this subject we glean a few extracts from his discussion of the three kingdoms:

> The gates of admission into these three kingdoms is different —Flesh, Faith, and Works. To be born of the flesh, or to be a descendant of Abraham, introduced a child into the first kingdom of God. To be born of water and spirit, through

---

[10] *The Christian Baptist*, VI, 557-8. April,1829.

faith in Jesus Christ, brings men and women into the second kingdom. But neither flesh, faith, nor water, without good works, will introduce a man or woman into the third kingdom.

The nature of these three kingdoms, the privileges enjoyed by the subjects, and the terms of admission, are very imperfectly understood in the present day. These kingdoms are unhappily confounded in the minds of many.... All the descendants of Jacob, without regard to regeneration, were lawful subjects of the first kingdom. None can be subjects of the second unless born again; and flesh and blood cannot inherit the third and ultimate kingdom.... It is but an opinion that infants, idiots, and some Jews and Pagans may without even faith or baptism, be brought into the third kingdom, merely in consequence of the sacrifice of Christ; and I doubt not that many Paido-baptists of all sects will be admitted into the kingdom of glory. Indeed, all they who obey Jesus Christ, through faith in his blood, according to their knowledge, I am of the opinion will be introduced into that kingdom....

There are three kingdoms: the kingdom of the Law, the Kingdom of Favor, and the Kingdom of Glory; each has a different constitution, different subjects, privileges, and terms of admission.... But when we speak of admission into the everlasting kingdom, we must have due respect to those grand and fundamental principles so clearly propounded in the New Institution. We must discriminate between the kingdom of favor and the kingdom of glory. . (He then spoke at length as if in vision he were speaking as one who had passed from life to the realm of the departed.)

When I waited at the altar and waited in the sanctuary my conscience was often troubled. I saw that His institution differed from that of Moses as the sun excelled a star. I apprehended the reign of favor, and gladly became a citizen of the

> second kingdom.... I felt myself in a new kingdom, a kingdom of favor. Sin did not now lord it over me as before, and my heart beat in unison with the favor which super, abounded; so that in comparison with the former kingdom, my sun always shone in a bright and cloudless sky.
>
> I ran the race and finished my course. I slept in Jesus; and lo! I awoke at the second trump, and all my deeds came into remembrance, not one of them was forgotten by God.
>
> The contrast between the kingdom of law and the kingdom of favor prepared me to enjoy and to relish the contrast between the kingdom of favor and the kingdom of glory.
>
> I have been thrice born—once of flesh, once of water and spirit, and once from the grave. Each birth brought me into congenial society. My fellow citizens always resembled my nativity. I was surrounded once with the children of the flesh, then with those born from above, and now with those born from the ashes of the grave.

Yes, this great revelation was the straw that broke the Campbell back and turned their angry agents against the Mormon leaders. Their historian Hayden later wrote of conditions in Hiram at this critical time:

> Perhaps in no place, except Kirtland, did the doctrines of the "Latter-day Saints" gain a more permanent footing than in Hiram. It entrenched itself there so strongly that its leaders felt.assured of the capture of the town. Rigdon's former popularity in that region gave wings to their appeal, and many people, not avowed converts, were under a spell of wonder at the strange things sounded in their ears.[11]

This great revelation did much to encourage and unite the

---

[11] Hayden, *op. cit.*, p. 216.

Saints as it turned the enemy against them. Its value was well expressed by the Prophet in these words:

> Nothing could be more pleasing to the Saints upon the order of the kingdom of the Lord, than the light which burst upon the world through the foregoing vision. Every law, every commandment, every promise, every truth, and every point touching the destiny of man, from Genesis to Revelation, where the purity of the scriptures, remains unsullied by the folly of men, go to show the perfection of the theory (of different degrees of glory in the future life) and witness the fact that that document is a transcript from the records of the eternal world. The sublimity of the ideas; the purity of the language; the scope for action; the continued duration for completion, in order that the heirs of salvation may confess the Lord and bow the knee; the rewards for faithfulness, and the punishments for sins, are so much beyond the narrow-mindedness of men, that every honest man is constrained to exclaim: "It came from God!"

A Coat of Tar and Feathers

As this good news was noised abroad the enemy resolved to put the work down with a cruel hand. In fact they carefully planned to kill the two leaders. During a cold spell in March their wicked plan was to be carried out. A physician in the town contributed two vials of poison, one to kill the Johnson watch dog, the other to be forced down the throats of the men. Some of the poison was inserted in a piece of meat and fed to the dog. The great watch dog, Rover, was cold and silent when the men were ready for their well planned party. In the day time while the Johnson house was vacant, Eli Johnson and John Ural entered the house, spiked the Johnson guns so they could not be used against them when they should attack the inmates that evening. They even stole one of Joseph's pillows so they could use the feathers to throw upon him after they covered his body with warm tar.

Everything in readiness, the guns spiked, the dog poisoned, the tar and feathers ready, the son of a "Campbellite" minister McClentic, living near Rigdon's house, gave a barrel of whiskey to the mobbers when they were ready to kill the two leaders.[12] On a very cold night, after a round of drinks, the enemy was at the door of the Johnson home. There was no barking dog to sound the alarm and no weapons in the house to be used against them. These drunken fiends seized the Prophet, dragging him from his bed and carried him out into the bitter cold. Several men had their hands upon him at once until they reached the door, where only two or three could find room to hold him in their grasp.

At the doorway he broke loose and seized the largest and strongest man in the crowd, Warren Waste, a trained wrestler who was considered the strongest man on the Western Reserve. Before the crowd could seize the Prophet again he threw his full strength against Waste, but his energy was only wasted, as the gang was soon upon him. Waste later said that "Joe Smith was the strongest man I ever grappled with."

Some of his clothes were torn from his body and he was dragged into the orchard back of the house. An open vial of poison was thrust against his lips, but he kept his mouth closed so no poison would get into it. The small bottle was beaten against his teeth until it was broken, its sharp edges cutting his lips severely.

He was beat unconscious, covered with a coat of warm tar and left for dead. When his friends carried him back to the house he was told that Sidney Rigdon had received the same treatment. He had been dragged over the frozen plowed ground until he was soon knocked unconscious and serious injury was done to the base of his

---

[12] *Church History (Reorganized)*, I, 243.

skull. Many people blame this accident for his future delinquency in the Church. While in Liberty Jail he acted like a mad man and was released.

The next day, being the Sabbath, the Prophet kept a preaching appointment in the village. In the audience were some of the mobbers and the men who helped plan the crime.

Within a few years all the men who took part in that raid had suffered a painful death. Miles Norton who poisoned the Johnson watch dog was killed by a ram in the barnyard, its spiral horn being thrust through Norton's body. Warren Waste and Carnot Mason boasted of having bent the Prophet's legs over his back, holding them in that position as he lay on the ground face downward. Waste was later killed by a falling log while he was building a house. Mason died from a spinal affliction that was more painful than a Boston Crab. The man who tried to pour the poison into his mouth was buried alive while digging a well.

At that time the adopted Murdock twins were suffering from the measles. The little boy was very sick, the girl having practically recovered. On that particular night the boy was sleeping with the Prophet so that Emma could get some sleep. When the Prophet was dragged from his bed the little boy was left uncovered, caught a severe cold and soon died. This child may well be called the first martyr in this dispensation.

This was the price Joseph Smith had to pay for spending a winter in Hiram, the hotbed of the "Campbellites," some of whom had apostatized from the Church.

The "Disciples" were so delighted to welcome Symonds Ryder and his colleagues back into their society that he was honored with many positions of trust and responsibility as a reward for his return. In 1843 he employed Abraham Lincoln to institute a chancery suit in the courts, receiving several letters from the young lawyer who was destined to become the great emancipator.[13]

Almost forty years after the incident, Ryder was invited to write an account of Joseph Smith's activity in Hiram during that historic winter. His epistle included these lines:

> To give particulars of the Mormon excitement of 1831 would require a volume-a few words must suffice. It has been stated that from the year 1815 to 1835, a period of twenty years, "all sorts of doctrine by all sorts of preachers had been heard;" and most of the people of Hiram had been disposed to turn out and hear. This went by the specious name of "liberal." The Mormons in Kirkland, being informed of this peculiar state of things, were soon prepared for the onset.
>
> In the winter of 1831 Joseph Smith, with others, had an appointment in the south school-house, in Hiram. Such was the apparent piety, sincerity and humility of the speakers, that many of the hearers were greatly affected, and thought it impossible that such preachers should lie in wait to deceive.
>
> During the next spring and summer several converts were made, and their success seemed to indicate an immediate triumph in Hiram. But when they went to Missouri to lay the foundation of the splendid city of Zion, and also of the temple, they left their papers behind. This gave their new converts an opportunity to become acquainted with the internal arrangement of their church, which revealed to them the horrid fact that a plot was laid to take their property from them and place it under the control of Joseph Smith the prophet. This was too much for the Hiramites, and they left the Mormonites faster than they had ever joined them, and by fall the Mormon church in Hiram was a very lean concern.

---

[13] P. M. Angel, *New Letters and Papers of Abraham Lincoln*, p. 18.

> But some who had been the dupes of this deception, determined not to let it pass with impunity; and, accordingly, a company was formed of citizens from Shalersville, Garretsville, and Hiram, in March, 1832, and proceeded to headquarters in the darkness of night, and took Smith and Rigdon from their beds, and tarred and feathered them both, and let them go. This had the desired effect, which was to get rid of them. They soon left for Kirtland.
>
> All who continued with the Mormons, and had any property, lost all; among whom was John Johnson, one of our most worthy men; also, Esq. Snow, of Mantua, who lost two or three thousand dollars.[14]

It was a high price they were asked to pay for a few months in Hiram, but it was well worth the cost. The one majestic revelation of the three degrees of glory repaid them for all their efforts, and hardships in that village. It is one of the greatest contributions ever made in the world of religious philosophy.

Was the Revision Completed?

At this point we should say that the revision was continued until July 2, 1833, at which time it was completed, at least for the time. Five months before that date the revision of the New Testament had been finished. When the labor was at an end the brethren "returned gratitude to our heavenly. Father." Even before the task was terminated there had been much discussion about printing the revision. On June 25, 1833, the First Presidency explained, "In regard to the printing of the New Translation: it cannot be done until we can attend to it ourselves, and this we will do as soon as the Lord permits."

It is not unlikely that this was an initial, preliminary revision,

---

[14] Hayden, *op. cit.*, pp.216-219

the Prophet intending to make further changes in the future. George Q. Cannon explains that "the inspired translation was completed for the time being." The same reliable authority heard Brigham Young state that "the Prophet had spoken to him about going through the translation of the scriptures again and perfecting it upon points of doctrine which the Lord had restrained from giving in plainness and fullness at the time of which we write."[15]

He also insisted that "it is not the will of the Lord to print any of the New Translation in the *Evening and Morning Star*, but when it is published it will all go to the world together."[16] He expressed a desire to publish the revised "New Testament and the Book of Mormon together."

Six months after the revision was completed the Prophet wrote to the Saints in Missouri, explaining that the Lord had not revealed to him "why God has suffered so great a calamity to come upon Zion." While engaged in the revision of the Apocalypse he was inspired to make many changes in the early chapters,[17] yet he did not explain chapter 12 and 13 which deal with Zion's bondage and redemption.

Later he was given a vast amount of information on that subject.[18] It is not unlikely that he received much information after 1833 which he wished to incorporate later in his revision. On June 18, 1840, seven years after his initial revision was completed, he recorded in his diary, "The time has come when Joseph should commence the work of translating the Egyptian Records, the Bible, etc."[19]

For five years he had been translating the Egyptian records. A few months later they were preparing "cuts" and assembling material for the printing of the "Book of Abraham." This refer-

---

[15] George Q. Cannon, *Life of Joseph Smith*, p. 142.
[16] *Times and Seasons*, V, 754.
[17] Doctrine and Covenants, Section 77.
[18] Doctrine and Covenants, Sections 101, 103, 105, and 106.
[19] *History of the Church*, IV, 137.

ence at that late day applied to the revision of the Bible more than it did to the Egyptian papyrus, since the latter was largely completed by that time.

During the last few years of the Prophet's life he often quoted texts from the Bible and then translated them in plainer language. In 1842 he quoted the popular text in Malachi about the coming of Elijah, and then explained, "I might have rendered a plainer translation to this but it is sufficiently plain to suit my purpose as it stands."[20]

He often quoted texts from the Bible and then corrected them, his correction not having been included in his preliminary revision.[21] Long after the revision is said to have been finished he said, "There are many things in the Bible that do not, as they now stand, accord with the revelations of the Holy Ghost to me."[22]

Many changes had been made in most of the books of the Bible. The last ones in the Old Testament, however, were revised very slightly. When they turned to the "Song of Solomon," Sidney wrote the title at the top of the page as was his custom. He then wrote these words as the Prophet dictated them, "This book is not inspired scripture." They turned to the next book and resumed the revision. This was the only book excluded from his revision.

After the death of Joseph Smith, President Brigham Young was unable to recover the manuscript and Bible which had been used during the revision. However, he did retain the duplicate manuscript which had been made by Dr. John M. Bernhisel and the Bible in which he had copied all the check marks that appeared in the original. After the loss of the 116 pages of the Book of Mormon manuscript the Prophet always made duplicate copies of all important material.

In 1867 the Reorganized Church published the inspired revi-

---

[20] Doctrine and Covenants 128:18.
[21] *History of the Church*, IV, 602; V, 343; VI, 184.
[22] Ibid., V, 424.

sion of the Bible. The "Words of Moses" and the "Prophecy of Enoch" appear at the beginning of Genesis. Many recent scholars have praised Joseph Smith for having the courage to cast the "Song of Solomon" from the collection, yet such a daring procedure would have been regarded as blasphemy in 1833, except in communities where the "Campbellite" philosophy was well known.

One famous minister has said of this revision:

> One of the most puzzling Bibles in print is that published in 1867 by the Reorganized Latter-day Saints. It has many additions to the text, Joseph Smith having claimed revelations for the changes made. Had these changes favored the doctrinal positions of his church the explanations would have been easy, but they do not seem to serve any denominational or sectarian purpose....
>
> It must be said that he had the courage deliberately to alter the text, and to make it say clearly what many Bible students succed in getting by theological legerdemain....[23]

The revision completed, the prophet was now free to. devote his full time to the ministry. This task had occupied most of his spare time for more than three years. Its completion was followed by a period of doctrinal development and growth in ecclesiastical pattern.

---

[23] Marion P. Simms, *The Bible from the Beginning*, p. 293.

Chapter XIV

AN ERA OF DOCTRINAL DEVELOPMENT

During the few months that the Prophet resided in Hiram, Ohio, he received fifteen revelations. While visiting in Kirtland during that winter he received two additional revelations and one in Amherst and another in Orange, Ohio while on a visit to those towns.

As soon as springtime opened the portals of the canals and turnpikes, Joseph Smith and a few friends were on their way to Missouri. Soon after their arrival in that historic land he received two revelations that were filled with information concerning Zion and her stakes.[1]

When the Prophet returned to Kirtland he continued the revision of the Bible, yet devoted much time to building up the Church and advancing the ministry. The first revelation he received after returning to Kirtland is that masterpiece on Priesthood which now appears in Section 84.

Among the many revelations that were given at this time in answer to prayer was the remarkable prophecy on war. At the close of the year 1832 there was much talk in the land about the southern states withdrawing from the Union. In November of that year South Carolina had declared the tariff laws of 1828 and 1832 not binding within that state. The northern states were anxious to

---

[1] Doctrine and Covenants, Sections 82 and 83.

raise a military force and compel the southern states to become loyal to the Union.

The newspapers were filled with accounts of the widening breach between the states. William Miller, Alexander Campbell, and others in Ohio were declaring that the end of the world was at hand. On Christmas day the Prophet prayed for information on the subject and received that marvelous revelation and prophecy regarding the Civil War.[2]

Joseph Smith was never anxious to rush anything into print in order to exhalt or magnify him as a prophet or magnify him in the eyes of his friends. To the contrary, he was always reluctant to do that. Though he was translating the Egyptian papyri as early as 1835, he did not have it in print until 1842. This prophecy on war could have been rushed to Independence, Missouri and published in the Book of Commandments, or it could have been published in a leaflet immediately and circulated in vast numbers, but it did not appear in the edition of 1833 nor the larger compilation two years later. In fact Joseph Smith never saw that prophecy in print.

The Prophet was in his grave for seven years before the great prophecy on war was published to the world. At that time it was not printed in the Doctrine and Covenants, but in the first edition of the Pearl of Great Price. Not until 1876 did it find a place in the Doctrine and Covenants.

This remarkable prophecy was revealed on Christmas day, 1832. Two days later the Prophet received that historic document which is preserved in Section 88. When he mailed a copy of this document to a friend he called it the "Olive Leaf which we have plucked from the tree of Paradise, the Lord's message of peace to us."

The Word of Wisdom

In the winter of 1833 the School of the Prophets met in Kirtland

---

[2] Doctrine and Covenants, Section 87.

for instruction. For a time they assembled in a small room in the home of Newel K. Whitney. Joseph Smith's family were again guests in that welcome home after they had been obliged to leave Hiram. It was then a common practice for most men to smoke or chew tobacco. When the small class room became filled with tobacco smoke it made an unsuitable place in which to study. The room, directly above the Smith kitchen, was a small one and was always filled to capacity. During that cold season of the year it was impossible to open the windows for ventilation, thus it became very unsuitable for prayerful meditation and serious reflection.

It was Emma's responsibility to keep the room clean, and it became a source of inconvenience and unnecessary labor to sweep up the burned tobacco that had been shaken from their pipes, the cigarette stubs, and the brown pools of tobacco juice that had missed the metal targets on the floor.

Coming in from the fresh, crisp February air the class room presented an unwholesome atmosphere. Perhaps others besides Emma had suggested that the brethren abstain from the use of tobacco while in the class room, but the Prophet was a tender hearted and sympathetic man, anxious not to offend or make one student feel un welcome. For this reason he refused to announce that the use of tobacco would not be tolerated in the class until he first earnestly prayed about the matter.

President Brigham Young, Zebedee Coltrin, and other witnesses have related that when the Prophet entered the room he "often found himself in a cloud of tobacco smoke and the floor soiled." When he prayed about this subject the "Word of Wisdom" was given as an answer.[3]

It is said that when the Prophet read the document to the class that they accepted it as the will of the Lord.

One of the students arose, took his hat and passed it among

---

[3] Doctrine and Covenants, Section 89.

the members. They placed in the hat their supplies of tobacco and pipes. He then opened the door of the stove and emptied the collection of forbidden articles into the fire. Coltrin asserts that he never smoked again after hearing the revelation read to the members of the class, but some of the brethren found the habit very difficult to break.

Yes, they were not to use tobacco in the classroom—or anywhere else. This document has proved to be a worthy monument to the inspiration of Joseph Smith.

In the months that followed, many revelations were given while the Prophet resided in Kirtland, all of which were given at a time of crisis and as a solution to some pressing problem. Following this important message, ten revelations were subsequently given in Kirtland. In the autumn of 1833 the Prophet went on a short missionary tour with Sidney Rigdon and a new convert named Freeman Nickerson. The latter had invited these men to accompany him to his home in Perrysburg, New York. They arrived at that place on the twelfth day of October, at which time another revelation was received.[4]

The Prophet was soon back in Kirtland, where the next four revelations were received. During the journey of Zion's Camp another revelation was given.[5] Upon his return to Kirtland the next six revelations were given at that place. Section 111 was given in Salem, Massachusetts during a missionary journey to the East. In the summer of 1837 another one was received in Kirtland, which was the last one given in that city.[6]

The following eleven sections of the Doctrine and Covenants were given in the land of Missouri during the last months the Saints spent in that land of opposition. The history covering that period of time and its relation to the revelations that were given at

---

[4] Doctrine and Covenants, Section 100.
[5] Doctrine and Covenants, Section 105.
[6] Doctrine and Covenants, Section 112.

The Law of Tithing

At Far West, Missouri, July 8, 1838, the law of tithing was revealed.[7] This was given as a substitute for the law of consecration which was not practiced by many of the branches, and which was not adequate during that era of bitter persecution to take care of the poor members of the Church.

In 1834 Joseph Smith and Oliver Cowdery covenanted with the Lord that they would give one-tenth of all their possessions, to be bestowed upon the poor. There had been no command to make such a contribution, but they were likely inspired to do so after reading how Jacob and others in ancient Israel had made such a covenant. Their pledge is so interesting that we present it in full:

> That if the Lord will prosper us in our business and open the way before us that we may obtain means to pay our debts, that we be not troubled nor brought into disrepute before the world, nor His people; after that, of all that He shall give unto us we will give a tenth to be bestowed upon the poor in His Church, or as he shall command; and that we will be faithful over that which he has entrusted to our care, that we may obtain much; and that our children after us shall remember to observe this sacred and holy covenant, and that our children, and our children's children may know of the same.

It was a time of persecution and poverty for the Saints in Missouri. Persecution had followed them through six counties in that state. It was the eve of the bitter strife that culminated in the "Battle of Crooked River," the Haun's Mill massacre, and a season of house burnings, brutal beatings, imprisonments, and perse-

---

[7] Doctrine and Covenants, Section 119.

cution that drove them from their homes, leaving them without money or even the bare necessities of life.

Moreover, many of the Saints who were coming to Missouri at that time had experienced similar distress elsewhere and were headed for Zion in a penurious condition. On the sixth day of July, 1838, Joseph Smith received a letter from his brother, Don Carlos, from a place "nine miles from Terre Haute, Indiana," informing him that a small party of the Saints, including his father and mother and two married sisters were on their way from Kirtland to Missouri. This epistle reveals the plight of the ones who were on their way to Zion and is typical of the condition of the Saints in Missouri. Everybody was in dire distress. It was a time when something must be done to relieve the poverty of the Saints and make ample provision for the future financial stability of the, growing society. This letter, which reveals the spirit and atmosphere of the time, contained the following account of their hardships:

> We have left two horses by the way sick, and a third horse (our main dependence) was taken lame last evening, and is not able to travel and we have stopped to doctor him. We were disappointed on every hand, before we started, in getting money. We got no assistance whatever, only as we have taken in Sister Singley, and she has assisted us as far as her means extend. We had, when we started, $75 in money. We sold the two cows for $13.50 per cow. We have sold of your goods to the amount of $45.74, and now we have only $25 to carry twenty-eight souls and thirteen horses, five hundred miles.
>
> We have lived very close and camped out at night, notwithstanding the rain and cold, and my baby only two weeks old when we started. Agnes is very feeble; father and mother are not well, and very much fatigued; mother has a severe cold,

and in fact, it is nothing but the power of faith and power of God, that will sustain them and bring them through. Our courage is good, and I think we shall be brought through. I leave it to you and Hyrum to devise some way to assist us to some more expense money. We have unaccountably bad roads, had our horses down in the mud, and broke one wagon tongue and thills, and broke down the carriage twice, and yet we are all alive and encamped on a dry place for almost the first time. Poverty is a very heavy load, but we 'are all obliged to welter under it.

It is now dark and I close. May the Lord bless you all and bring us together is my prayer. Amen. All the arrangements that Brother Hyrum left for getting money failed; they did not gain us one cent.

It certainly grieved the Prophet to learn that his parents, two of his married sisters and his beloved brother, Don Carlos, were in such a sad plight. As the enemy was making final preparations to drive the Mormons from their land of Zion, the Prophet was deeply concerned about the financial condition of his people. Two days after the epistle from Don Carlos was received, the Prophet prayed, "O Lord show unto thy servants, how much thou requirest of the properties of thy people for a tithing." The word "tithing" is here used in its larger sense and is not restricted to its narrower meaning of one-tenth. In answer to his inquiry the great revelation on tithing was received. On the eve of the exodus from Missouri and the building of Nauvoo, it was given at a very appropriate time.

Sections 121, 122, and 123 were written by the Prophet during his long imprisonment in Liberty Jail in Clay County, Missouri. These were the last ones written in Missouri. They are impressive monuments to the inspiration of the man who wrote them. They serve as a fitting climax to the history of the Saints in the land where Adam dwelt, They are Joseph Smith's valedictory to his enemies, to the Saints, and to the world. These epistles from prison have a spirit that is divine. They are as well known to the members of the Church as are any other chapters in that book of modern scripture.

At the time of the exodus from Missouri one hundred thirty-five chapters in the word of God to this generation had been recorded. Twenty of them had been recorded in Missouri, sixty-four in Ohio, fifteen in Pennsylvania, twenty-five in New York, and one in Massachusetts. The doctrinal foundations of the growing society were well laid by the time the Saints fled from their enemies in Missouri, yet some precious documents were soon to be added to the collection.

PART III

THE ILLINOIS CHAPTER IN THE WORD OF GOD

Chapter XV

REVELATION IN ILLINOIS

Ten of the Sections of the Doctrine and Covenants were recorded in Illinois, all of them being given in Nauvoo except Sections 130 and 131, which were revealed in the neighboring town of Ramus. In that community there was a small branch of the Church for several years and the Prophet made a few visits to the village and later wrote a few letters to friends who lived there.

During this visit the Prophet and William Clayton stayed with Benjamin F. Johnson who lived in that community. While a guest in the Johnson home he explained to his friends that "except a man and his wife enter into an everlasting covenant and be married for eternity, while in this probation, by the power and authority of the holy Priesthood, they will cease to increase when they die; that is, they will not have any children after the resurrection."

The first revelation given in Illinois is preserved in Section 124, and was given January 19, 1841. By that time the mission of Elijah was unfolding to the mind of the Prophet and the time was fully ripe to turn the keys of the sealing power of the Priesthood. At that time a flood of inspiration had burst upon the Prophet's mind regarding this important feature of the restoration. He likely had a full knowledge of how the temple would be constructed and what ceremonies would be conducted within its many rooms.

More is said in this revelation concerning the purposes of temples than has since been published to the world, which is evidence that he had a wealth of information on the subject before work was commenced on the temple. In the months that followed, the Prophet became fearful that, his life might be taken before the temple was completed, so he decided to give the endowment ceremony to a few of his intimate friends long before the temple was finished. That historic occasion was the fourth day of May, 1842.[1]

Though the temple was not finished when the Prophet and his brother were martyred, it was completed before the Saints left Nauvoo and about 2,000 of them received their endowments before they left the city. No endowments for the dead were given in Nauvoo.

The next chapter in the word of God to this generation was given in response to this question, "What is the will of the Lord concerning the Saints in the Territory of Iowa?" The next message was a brief one addressed to Brigham Young, advising him to remain with his family and not devote his full time to the ministry abroad. This short chapter has about ten words more than Section 13, which is the shortest one in the volume.

In the latest edition the Appendix retains its position near the close of the volume. It is followed by an account of the martyrdom of Joseph and Hyrum Smith. The last chapter in the collection is the revelation given to President Brigham Young concerning the organization of the camps of Israel in preparation for their journey across the plains.

The Prophet in Exile

It was a time of sorrow when the Prophet's enemies were search-

---

[1] For a complete discussion of this subject the reader is invited to read the author's book. *Mormonism and Masonry*, pp. 122-150, and *Nauvoo the Beautiful*, pp. 96-120.

ing for him and he was obliged to flee from the city and spend weeks in exile. In order, to escape his foes he would spend a few days in the home of a friend and then be taken secretly to another place. For a season he lived on a small island in the Mississippi, and with friends along the Iowa shore. He was a tender hearted, affectionate man who enjoyed the friendship of his family and associates, dreading the days that would separate them. It was always a time of trial to be separated from his wife and children, living in seclusion for weeks at a time.

Every letter he ever wrote to his family reveals the deep love he had for them and how it broke his heart to be separated from them.

As a missionary in New York City in 1832, he wrote a long letter to his wife, which contained this paragraph which speaks the secrets of his heart:

> ...I returned to my room to meditate and calm my mind, and behold the thoughtful home of Emma and Julia rushes upon my mind like a flood and I could wish for a moment to be with them. My breast so fills with all the feelings and tenderness of a parent and husband, and could I be with you I would tell you many things....
>
> I prefer reading and praying and holding communion with the Holy Spirit and writing to you, than walking the streets and beholding the distraction of men....
>
> I hope you will excuse me for writing so soon after writing for I feel as if I wanted to say something to comfort you in your peculiar trial and present affliction.

While in exile he wrote a long letter to his wife, containing this paragraph which is typical of all his letters:

> Tell the children it is well with their father, as yet; and that

> he remains in fervent prayer to Almighty God for the safety of himself, and for you, and for them.
>
> Tell Mother Smith that it shall be well with her son, whether in life or in death, for thus saith the Lord God; tell her that I remember her all the while, as well as Lucy, and tell the rest, that all must be of good cheer.

As a prisoner in a Missouri dungeon he wrote these lines to his wife:

> O, God grant that I may have the privilege of seeing once more my lovely family, in the enjoyment of the sweets of liberty and social life; to press them to my bosom and kiss their lovely cheeks would fill my heart with unspeakable gratitude. Tell the children I am alive and trust I shall come and see them before long. Comfort their hearts all you can; and try to be comforted yourself, all you can....
>
> Tell little Joseph he must be a good boy. Father loves him with a perfect love. He is the eldest, and must not hurt those that are smaller than him, but must comfort them. Tell little Frederick father loves him with all his heart. He is a lovely boy. Julia is a lovely little girl; I love her also. She is a promising child; tell her father wants her to remember him and be a good girl. Tell all the rest that F think of them and pray for them all.

It was always a source of sorrow to this tender hearted man to be away from his family and friends. In the autumn of 1842 he was in seclusion again yet he yearned to be with the Saints and preach to them the wealth of new information he had received on the subject of temple work and baptism for the dead. For a season they had been experimenting in that field, but now he had been told the true path to follow. They had been careless in recording all the baptisms they had performed and they even baptized men for women and women in behalf of men. Such mistakes were not to be continued.

While in exile he had ample time to think of his family and friends. He longed to be with the Saints and preach to them in their large assemblies. He was not content merely to write letters to his wife and children, reminding them of his love and concern for them, but he wanted to write to all the members of the Church, writing them sermons that would be read in their crowded assemblies and finally included in the collection of the word of God to this generation.

In exile he had ample time to meditate and pray about the things of the kingdom. During this season of exile and loneliness he received a flood of revealed wisdom on the subject of baptism for the dead and temple work in general. The last day in August he spoke to the members of the Relief Society, explaining that "a few very important things have been manifested to me in my absence respecting the doctrine of baptisms for the dead, which I shall communicate to the Saints next Sabbath, if nothing should occur to prevent me."

He did not tarry in the city until the next Sabbath, however, but was obliged to flee soon after he preached this sermon to the women of Nauvoo. Fearful that he would not be in attendance at the Sabbath meeting he wrote some of his thoughts on the subject, sending the epistle by special messenger to Nauvoo where it should be read in small circles of friends and in their Sabbath services, and finally be included in the collection of the word of God and go forth to all the world for all people to read until the end of time.

A few days later he wrote another epistle on the same subject. These two epistles were considered worthy of a permanent place in the sacred records of the Church. They are preserved in Sections 127 and 128 of the Doctrine and Covenants.

The Revelation on Celestial Marriage

As early as 1831 it had been made known to Joseph Smith that plural marriage would be made a feature of the dispensation of the fullness of times. At that early date he secretly explained the new doctrine to some of the leaders of the Church and for years it was secretly discussed by them. In the course of time the information spread beyond the official circles of the Church and fell upon the ears of the enemy. At that early date it was doubtless made known that in the near future many important keys would be restored-keys of the ancient dispensations, a feature of which was the practice of plural marriage.

Elder Orson Pratt preached a sermon during the October conference in 1869, in which he declared that the Prophet had declared these fats to his intimate friends while he was residing in the Johnson home in Hiram, Ohio. While a guest in the Johnson home he was devoting most of his time to a study of the scriptures, revising the Old Testament. It is probable that while studying the lives of the great patriarchs of Israel that he inquired of the Lord to know more about that principle. He then received the full explanation, but did not have it recorded at the time.

It is evident that this subject was widely discussed by the leaders of the Church in the coming years. It soon reached beyond the officials of the Church and was spread broadcast by the enemy. It is surprising at what an early date the Mormons were accused of preaching the doctrine of plural marriage. The enemy knew that the doctrine was being discussed as early as 1832. It certainly did not first fall upon the ears of the enemy in far away Utah, nor in Nauvoo, nor in Missouri, but soon after the Saints went to Ohio.

The fact that the enemy had so much to say about the subject is proof that the leaders of the Church were discussing it extensively at the time.

At an early time the Elder's Journal and other official publications of the Church sought to correct this misunderstanding, assuring the public that they were not preaching or practicing plural marriage. The enemies in Ohio and Missouri have left an unimpeachable witness that plural marriage was being discussed by the leaders of the Church, but it was their understanding that it had simply been explained at that early date, but would not be practiced until some future date.

By 1835 this doctrine had been so widely discussed in the Church and out of the Church, and so much had been said about this being one of the teachings of the Latter-day Saints, that an article on the subject appeared at the close of the Doctrine and Covenants. This was not a regular revelation, but was written at that time of crisis in order to clarify the position of the Church regarding that widely discussed subject.

"Inasmuch as this Church has been reproached with the crime of fornication and polygamy," it recalled, "we believe that one man should have one wife; and one women but one husband, except in case of death, when either is at liberty to marry again."

To our misinformed friends who insist that plural marriage was first taught and practiced in Utah, we would ask why this paragraph should be inserted in the 1835 edition of the Doctrine and Covenants if the Church leaders had not been discussing the subject for a few years and the information had not spread far and wide?

Since the article on marriage does not appear in recent editions of the Doctrine and Covenants we shall quote two paragraphs from this article:

> It is not right to persuade a woman to be baptized contrary to the will of her husband. All children are bound by law to obey their parents; and to influence them to embrace any religious faith, or to be baptized, or leave their parents without their consent is unlawful and unjust.
>
> Marriage should be celebrated with prayer and thanksgiving; and at the solemnization, the persons to be married, should stand together, the man on the right and the woman on the left, shall be addressed by the person officiating, as he shall be directed by the holy Spirit; and if there be no legal objections, he shall say, calling each by their names: "You both mutually agree to be each others companion, husband and wife, observing the legal rights belonging to this condition; that is, keeping yourselves wholly for each other, and from all others, during your lives.

As the Church expanded with the years and its theological pattern was completely fashioned, angels from heaven having restored the keys of ancient dispensations, the Prophet was instructed to put into practice the revelation he had received in 1831. It is perfectly natural that he would be reluctant to rush that revelation into print or even to make a manuscript copy of it at the time. Persecution was thrust upon them from every quarter without this subject as a climax to turn the enemy against them with increased fury.

For these wise reasons he refused to publish or even write the revolutionary doctrine, keeping it locked in his heart, discussing it with his brethren, yet dreading the day when he should be asked to put it into practice. In the city of Nauvoo that day finally dawned and the leaders of the Church were instructed secretly to take plural wives, keeping the doctrine from the world as much as possible. As an example of what a secret they sought to make it we must mention the journal of a member of the Quorum of the

Twelve who wrote a paragraph in his diary in code. During World War II his descendants gave the secret document to the intelligence department of the United States Navy to have it deciphered. It turned out to be a record of his plural marriages, in which women were sealed to him for "time and eternity."

The Prophet Joseph. Smith received much opposition from his wife regarding this subject. Since there was no written revelation authorizing it she seems to have regarded it as not divine. William Clayton has preserved an account of how this revelation came to be recorded. He was the Prophet's secretary at the time and was in the office above the store when Joseph and Hyrum entered the room on that historic day, July 12, 1843. They were discussing this subject when they entered the office, Hyrum insisting that "If you will write the revelation on celestial marriage I will take it and read it to Emma, and I believe I can convince her of its truth, and you will hereafter have peace." Joseph smiled and replied, "You do not know Emma as well as I do."

Hyrum repeated his request, begging him to call his secretary, get the seerstone, and dictate the revelation that had slumbered in his heart all these years. "I can convince any reasonable man or woman of its truth, purity, and heavenly origin," he assured him. The Prophet replied that he would not need the seerstone, as he remembered it so well that he could dictate it without the use of that instrument.

He then did as his brother had suggested, dictating as fast as Brother Clayton could write. When it was recorded he had the secretary read it to him, pronouncing it "correct." While Brother Clayton rested, his assistant was asked to make a duplicate copy of the document.

Hyrum returned to the office a few hours later, secured a copy of the long document and set out to convince Emma that this was a divine message, as binding upon the Saints as any other revelation. One tradition asserts that she seized the manuscript from Hyrum and burned it. Another account represents her as persuading her husband to give the copy to her, which she destroyed after he placed the copy in her hands.

The other copy, however, was not destroyed. Many of the leaders of the Church heard it read to them in Nauvoo, as did many of the apostates who later assisted in starting the Reorganized Church. It was certainly no secret to the editors of the *Nauvoro Expositer*. A score of newspapers in that neighborhood mentioned it soon after it was being read to small groups in Nauvoo. The doctrine of plural marriage and the eternity of the marriage covenant was well known to the editors of all the newspapers in that region before this revelation was recorded. It was certainly, no secret to the editors of the *Quincy Whig,* the *Sangamon Journal,* the *Illinois Register,* the *Peoria Democratic Press,* the *Warsaw Signal,* the *Burlington Hawkeye,* and many other newspapers.

It was not preached publicly, however, until 1852, at which time Orson Pratt preached a long sermon on the subject and read the revelation.

This historic document was published in the 1876 edition of the Doctrine and Covenants. Since the time had arrived for the Saints to practice the celestial law it naturally repealed the former announcement on the subject. For this reason the article on marriage that was inserted in the 1835 edition was removed from the volume when the long revelation on celestial and plural marriage was inserted. Since that article of about four hundred words did not then express the teachings of the Church after its full theological pattern had been established, it was a natural and wise course to take out Section 101 and replace it with Section 132.

This revelation, like all others, came in answer to prayer, the question doubtless having been occasioned during his inspired revision of the bible. "Inasmuch as you have inquired of my hand to know and understand," it commences, bearing evidence that the Prophet sought divine assistance on this question. The answer was such a surprise that one need not be alarmed because he did not print it immediately or even have it written. Fearful of the persecution it would likely engender, he wisely chose to keep it a secret as long as he could.

Years later when the Saints were firmly entrenched in the tops of the mountains, away from their enemies, with all the ancient keys restored to the Church, it was an appropriate time to announce the doctrine in public and later to add the revelation to the Doctrine and Covenants.

The Doctrine and Covenants is the sacred book of the Latter-day Saints. Elder Osborne J. P. Widtsoe has wisely expressed it in these words:

> It meets conditions, not of two thousand years or more before Christ, but of the present day it gives specific directions for the establishing and maintaining of the Church of Christ, not among an oriental people in a primitive age, but among an active people in a progressive age. The living oracle of God is of far more value than the breathless letter.

The latest edition of this book of scriptures contains one hundred thirty-six chapters or Sections, the last one of which was given to Brigham Young. Nine of the others are not direct revelations in the usually accepted sense, but are minutes of important meetings, letters, addresses to the Saints, prayers and prophecies, and instructions which contain useful wisdom and a discussion of important doctrines. These chapters include Sections 102, 121, 123, 127, 128, 130, 131, 134, and 135.

The rest of the volume—126 Sections—are the revelations

Joseph Smith received for the Church or to individual members of the Church.

As the Doctrine and Covenants has gone forth to the world in many editions and languages, it has convinced many readers that it contains me word of God. When the book was first published it contained a "Testimony of the Twelve Apostles," bearing witness that the revelations were "given by divine inspiration." It contained this paragraph which thousands of readers have found to be true:

> We, therefore, feel willing to bear testimony to all the world of mankind, to every creature upon the face of the earth, that the Lord has borne record to our souls, through the Holy Ghost shed forth upon us, that these commandments were given by inspiration of God, and are profitable for all men and are verily true.

In this spirit the book has gone forth to the world, and in this spirit it has been received.

INDEX

A

Angel, Mary Ann, marries Brigham Young, 155

Anthon, Prof., Charles, is interviewed by Martin Harris, 15

Apocrypha, the, spoken of, 192-193

Apostacy, the, spoken of, 142-143

Article on Marriage in the 1835 edition of the Doctrine and Covenants, 223-224

Austin, Emily,l tells the story of the Colville Saints, 81-85

B

Baptist, John the, restores the Aaronic Priesthood, 42-43

Baptism for the dead explained, 220; discussed by the "Campbellites," 137

Benjamin, King, ascends the Nephite throne, 23

Bentley, Adamson, a "Campbellite" preacher and brother-in-law of sidney Rigdon, 101-116

Bible, revision of, by the "campbellites" 126-136; recommended by many authorities, 137; Inspired Revision of, by Joseph Smith, 175-195

Bidamon, Lewis C.,marries the widow of Joseph Smith, 30

Billings, Titus, deeds his property to the Church, 152

Book of Commandments, the, prepared for the press, 178-181

Book of Mormon, the, came from the press in March, 1830, 25; first edition contained a Preface about the lost manuscript, 27; two manuscripts made, 29; nearly 2,000,000 copies sold, 38; seven years required to sell first edition, 67

Booth, Ezra, apostatizes and becomes bitter enemy, 183, 196

Buchanan, Mrs., predicts end of the world, 91

C

Campbell, Alexander, pleads for a restoration, 99-146; speaks in defense of a revision of the Bible, 126-136; describes the three kingdoms, 197; leads the oppostion against Joseph Smith and Sidnet Rigdon, 196

"Campbellite" reformation, the, 99-146; their historians tell the story of the Mormons in Ohio, 114-124

Campbell, Thomas, starts a reformation, 100-110

Celestial Marriage, revelation concerning, 222

Christian Baptist, the, pleads for revision of the Bible, 138

Church, the, organized, 71

Clark, the Rev., John A., is intervoewed by Martin Harris, 19-20

Cobb, Mrs., one of the witnesses designated to see the Book of Mormon manuscript which Martin Harris wrote, 124

Colesville, New York, persecution in, 75-79; Colesville Saints go west, 80-85

Coltrin, Zebedee, speaks in tongues, 159; was present when the Word of wisdom was first read, 209

Commandments, Book of, the, prepared for publication, 177-181

Communistic societies, 145-151

Copley, Leman, gives a tract of land to the Church, 151; a missionary to the Shakers, 170

Cowdery, Lyman, a school teacher in western New York, 32

Cowdery, Oliver, a school teacher near Palmyra, 32; marries Elizabeth Ann Whitmer, 35; becomes the Prophet's scribe, 36; his later life, 44; his family, 44-46

Cutler, Alpheus, organizes a small faction, 78-79

D

Dibble, Philo, present when the vision about the three degrees of glory was given, 194

Dickensen's translation of the Bible quoted, 132

Discerning spirits, 158

"Disciples of Christ," the, 99-146

Doctrine and Covenants, the first edition of, 181

E

Errors in the Bible, 126-133; 169

Endowments given in Nauvoo, 217

Elect Lady, the, 59

Elijah, mission of, 217

F

Far West record, 157

Fox, George, the Quaker, 161

G

Gift of tongues, the, 154-158

H

Hale, Alva, drives to Palmyra to traansport Joseph and Emma to Harmony, 11

Hale, Issac, and his family, 2-12; his will, 8; his death, 8; unfriendly with Joseph Smith, 9; opposes the marriage of his daughter, 54-80; denounces Joseph Smith, 79-80

Harmony, Pennsylvania, the birthplace of Emma Hale, 6-16; Joseph Smith buys property there, 38

Harris, Martin, gives Joseph $50.00; visits Prof. Anthon, 15; becomes a scribe, 16; takes home the 116 pages he wrote, 17; loses the manuscript, 18; sells 150 acres to pay the printer, 67; is divorced, 66-68; marries caroline Young, 69; she takes their children to Utah, 68-70; he returns to the church, 69

Hiram, Ohio, scene of the conference that decided to publish the Book of Commandments, 178; the camp of the enemy, 183, 195, 200

Hulet Branch, the, spurious gift of tongues in, 157

Hymn books popular in all churches, 59

I

Icarians, the, start a communistic society in Nauvoo, 150

Ingersoll, Peter, told of Issac Hale's rebuke of Joseph smith, 79

Inspired Revision of the Bible made by Joseph Smith, 175-195

J

Jehoikim, King, burns a valuable document, 21

John the Baptist, retsores the keys of the Aaronic Priesthood, 43

K

Kimball, Sarah M., recovers a few pages of the original manuscript of the Book of Mormon, 30

King James Version of the Bible not perfect, 126-134

Knight, Joseph, a friend of the Smiths, 42; invites Joseph Smith to preach in his home, 74-76; discussed in Emily Austin's books, 80-84

Knight, Newel, is baptized, 73-74; casting the evil spirit from, 74; attends a confirmation service in Harmony 79

L

Laban, sword of, seen by the three witnesses, 67

Lamanite mission, 94

Lee, Ann, the Shaker leader, 161-173

Lewis, Nathaniel, Emma Smith's uncle, a preacher in Harmony, 5, 10-11; opposes Emma's marriage, 54-59

M

McLellin, William, objects to the literary style of the revelations, 177

Manuscript, the lost, 13-31

Markham, Edwin, mentions the Norm-Mother, 100

Marriage, Celestial, 222

Marsh, Thomas, B., 93; adised to beware, 159

Messenger and Advocate, the, publishes Oliver Cowdery's letter, 43

Millennial Harbinger, the, published in 1829; quoted from, 102, 106, 132,144

Miller, William, predicts the hour of Christ's return, 89-92

Missionaries to the Lamanites, the, four, 94

Morley, Issac, and the communistic society, the family, 146, 151

Mormon buries the gold plates, 24

N

Nauvoo House, Book of Mormon manuscript deposited in, 30

Norm-Mother, a Teutonic legend, 100

O

Olive Leaf, the, section, 82, 209

P

Page, Hiram, receives spurious revelations, 84-88

Partridge, Edward, visits the Prophet in New York, 94; assigns stewardships, 152-153; purchases lands in Missouri, 175

Pearl of Great Price, the, first published, 182

"Peepstone" of Hiram Page condemned, 85-89

Peter, James and John restore the keys to the Priesthood, 74, 96

Phelps, W. W., sees the Devil riding upon the waters, 168

Pratt, Orson, interviews david Whitmer, 31

Pratt, Parley P., a missionary to the Lamanites, 93; set apart for a mission to Canada, 99; goes on a mission to the Shakers, 169

Prophecy on the Civil War, 182

Prophecy of Enoch, the, 94

Q

Quakers, Shaking, the, 161-173

R

Rawlinson, George, expressed the hope that ancient sacred literature would be discovered, 40

Reorganized Church, the, has a complete copy of the Book of Mormon manuscript, 30; owns John whitmer's "History," 72

Restoration of the ancient Gospel expected by many, 103-110; "Restoration of the ancient order of things," 101-116

Rigdon, Sidney, visits Joseph Smith in New York, 94; a revelation given on his behalf, 108; had been a popular "Campbellite" preacher, 108-109; is condemned by the "Campbellites," 143; had long been in favor of "all things in common," 150; assisted in preparing the revelations for publication, 181; tarred and feathered, 200

Rockwell, O. P., joined the Church in New York, 95

Rothman speaks of the apostasy, 142

Ryder, Symonds, apostatizes and becomes a bitter enemy, 183, 196

S

Sacrament, the, instituted, water substituted for wine, 78

Salem, Massachusetts, a revelation given in, 211

Scott, Walter, a "Campbellite" minister, 101, 116

Simms, Dr. P. Marion, praises the Inspired Revision of the Bible, 192

Shakers, the, 161-173

Shinehah, the land of, 145

Small plates of Nephi, 22

Smith, Don Carlos, writes to the Prophet, 203

Smith, Emma, her family, 2-11; her marriage, 10; death of her first child, 24; descibes the gold plates, 41; returns to Harmony after the Church is organized, 54; is commanded to select hymns, 56-59; her final departure from Harmony, 79; a tribute paid to the Elect Lady, 59

Smith, Joseph, Sr., a revelation in his behalf, 41

Smith, Joseph, 107, poem of, 65

Smith, Samuel, took Oliver Cowdery to Harmony, 36-37

Smith, Vida E., poem of, 62

South Carolina, leads in the sucession movement, 208-209

Stoal, Josiah, employs Joseph Smith, 1; adises Emma to marry Joseph, 5; lived near the home of Joseph Knight, 5-6

Strang, James J., an apostate leader, 69

T

Tar and feathers for Joseph Smith and Sidney Rigdon, 200

Temple work discussed, 220-221

Thayer, Ezra, apostatizes, 159

Three kingdoms of glory, 193

Tithing, the law of, 212

Tolstoy objects to the king James Version, 190

Tongues, the gift of, 154-158

"Totonto Society," the, 99

Translation, the art of not fully explained, 42

Tyndale, William, translated the basic text of the King James Version, 131-132

U

"United Brethren," the, 99

"United Order," the, 110

Urim and Thummim, taken from Joseph Smith after the manuscript was lost, 24

V

Vision of glories, the 185-201

Voice of God, in the chambers of old father Whitmer, 75

Voice of Michael, 75

W

Wardley, James, starts the Shaker society, 161

Wassen, Elizabeth, Emma Smith's sister lived near Nauvoo, 9-11

Wassen, Lorenzo, Emma Smith's nephew, joins the Church, 9

Watson, John, explains the value of ancient parchment containing biblical writings, 39

Western Reserve, the, a place of preparation, 98-144

Words of Moses, the, 77, 94, 124

Whitmer, David, receives a testimony, 47-53; is interviewed by Orson Pratt and Joseph F. Smith, 55; sees the gold plates, 66-69; retained the traanscript of characters that Prof. Anthon examined, 15

Whitmer, Elizabeth Ann, marries Oliver Cowdery, 35

Whitmer, John, serves as historian, 71-72; visits Joseph Smith in Harmony, 77

Whitmer, Mrs. Peter, sees the gold plates, 52

Whitmer, Peter, fond of Oliver Cowdery, 35; invites Joseph and Oliver to finish the translation in his home, 48; miracles at his home, 47-49; Church organized in his home, 74

Widstoe, Osborne J. P., quoted, 227

Williams, Rodger, Pleads for a restoration, 143

Witnesses, three, the, see the plates, 66-70

Y

Young, Brigham, speaks in tongues, 155

Young, Caroline, marries Martin Harris, 69

Z

Zion's camp, 211

Zion, land of, 174-179